Thomas Wardlaw Taylor

The individual and the state;

An essay on justice

Thomas Wardlaw Taylor

The individual and the state;
An essay on justice

ISBN/EAN: 9783337858681

Printed in Europe, USA, Canada, Australia, Japan

Cover: Foto ©ninafisch / pixelio.de

More available books at **www.hansebooks.com**

THE

INDIVIDUAL AND THE STATE

AN ESSAY ON JUSTICE

A THESIS ACCEPTED BY THE FACULTY OF CORNELL
UNIVERSITY FOR THE DEGREE OF
DOCTOR OF PHILOSOPHY

BY

THOMAS WARDLAW TAYLOR, Jr., M.A.

BARRISTER AT LAW (MANITOBA) AND
LATE FELLOW OF THE SAGE SCHOOL OF PHILOSOPHY, CORNELL UNIVERSITY

BOSTON, U.S.A., AND LONDON
GINN & COMPANY, PUBLISHERS
1895

INDIVIDUAL AND THE STATE.

CHAPTER I.

I. THE RATIONALIZATION OF SOCIETY.

MAN first awakened to a consciousness of himself, not as an individual of indefinite worth, but simply as a member of a social group. In the earliest stages of his existence the only recognized bond for this union was a metaphysical one. Religion, in the form of manes worship, was the foundation of all primitive association.[1] Neither gregarious instinct nor the need of mutual assistance was the social bond of which men were conscious ; that was a unity of religious belief. Whether in the household, the clan, or, later, in the State, the acknowledgment of a common Eponym was necessary for union. All those who served the same Lares were members of the same family. The society thus organized consisted not merely of the living ; its membership included both the present and the past, both the living descendant and the deified ancestor. The gods were as truly members of the social group as were their worshippers. The god and his worshippers were bound together by the ties of human relationship ; together they made up one family, with reciprocal family duties.[2]

In such a society mere birth conferred no rights. Relationship was not measured by blood. Its standard was community of gods.[3] Its proof was subordination to a common authority.[4]

---

[1] De Coulanges, La Cité Antique; Hearn, Ancient Household; W. Robertson Smith, Religion of the Semites, Lect. II.
[2] The Religion of the Semites, Lect. II.
[3] La Cité Antique; Plato, Laws v. 729.
[4] Aryan Household, p. 66.

Kinship began and ended with the *patria potestas*.[1] The infant had no position in the household. A religious ceremony must take place before the child could become a member of the family.[2] The Father must accept it and present it to the spirits of the hearth. By virtue of the adoption the boy became a son, and in the same way the offspring of the stranger might attain to a sonship equally complete.[3]

The classical States were founded on the model of the household, both generally and in detail, and, like the household, were held together by the worship of the Eponym, whether god, or hero, or deified founder. Each clan and each family had its own deities and its own worship, but, over and beyond these, the common interests of the State demanded a common worship. Upon that worship the existence and all the functions of the State depended, and, if it failed, law, civic rights, and everything which depended upon it, failed also.[4] Within the narrow bounds of the religious community rights and duties were recognized ; outside those bounds the whole world were strangers, even enemies, from whom and with whom it was equally natural to plunder and to trade.

The Roman Empire did not materially affect that foundation. The Emperors, not satisfied with the dignity of Pontifex Maximus, found it necessary to deify themselves, and to arrogate to themselves the honors and powers of divinity. The deification of the Caesars was not an act of absurd adulation ; it was in perfect accord with all the pagan ideas of manes and hero worship. It was also of much greater importance than is usually supposed.[5] It has well been called the religious culmination of the ancient world. Whenever the Romans con- .

---

[1] Maine, Ancient Law, p. 149.

[2] Aryan Household, p. 72 ; La Cité Antique.

[3] Cf. Plato, Laws ix. 877, 878.

[4] Plutarch, Adv. Colotem, c. 31: "Sooner may a city exist without houses and ground than a city without faith in the gods. This is the bond of union, the support of all legislation."

[5] Upon the subject of Emperor worship, see Gerhard Uhlhorn, Conflict of Christianity with Heathenism, book I, chap. I, § 2.

quered a city or province, the local deities were invited, in a set formula, to desert the vanquished and to repair to Rome, where temples and games would be dedicated to their honor. Amidst this chaos of local religions there was felt need for some form of religious unity. Emperor worship supplied this unity. Through it was erected a great State church extending throughout the entire Empire, and exerting vast social and political influence, especially in the provinces. In many districts its priests exceeded in numbers and importance those of the local divinities, while it included amongst its adherents all loyal citizens. "Thus now existed, what hitherto had been unknown, a formal universal State religion in which it was the duty of the citizen to participate, and which he could not violate without committing, at the same time, a crime against the State. However tolerant one might be elsewhere, there could be no concession here."[1]

Like its predecessors, the unity of the Middle Ages was a religious one. Mediaeval Christendom was a theocracy.[2] It was not until the Church was firmly established as a governing power that anarchy gave place to law; it was not until the hierarchy had become the ruling force, that the struggle of warring fragments was replaced by a united Christendom.

In theory, the Pope, ruling as vicar of Christ, was at the head of the nations; his kingdom extended over all mankind; in his hands were both the spiritual and the temporal swords; he was the sovereign of the universe, the king of kings, and the princes of Europe were only his lieutenants.[3] Destructive as such a conception is to all national independence, and all individual liberty, this theory was, nevertheless, at that period, the only known guarantee of peace.[4] The Pope, as the supreme minister of a religion of peace and love, claimed the

---

[1] Uhlhorn, Conflict of Christianity with Heathenism, book I, chap. I, § 2.

[2] Laurent, l'Histoire de l'Humanité, tome VI, p. 23. Bryce, Holy Roman Empire, p. 88.

[3] Laurent, l'Histoire de l'Humanité, tome VI, p. 100.

[4] *Ibid.*, p. 247.

right to interfere in the quarrels of princes, to decide whether
wars were just or unjust, and to enforce his decision with all
the spiritual terrors at his command. Impelled by an instinct
of self-preservation, the kings constantly resisted or evaded
the enforcement of these claims; but not even the fiercest
Ghibelline would go further in his opposition to the Holy See
than to claim for the Empire an equality with it as the independent and divinely appointed temporal power.[1]

The religious character of that period is further evinced by
the interposition of the clergy in the administration of justice.
From the earliest days the Church had arbitrated in disputes
between its members. When, however, the Church had reached
the zenith of its power, ecclesiastical tribunals, sitting in complete independence of the royal courts, had sole jurisdiction
over all cases, both civil and criminal, in which clerics were
parties. This included all who were in any way connected
with the Church, whether they performed spiritual functions or
not. The numbers of these were greatly increased by the
indiscriminate granting of the tonsure, and by including the
multitudes who had vowed to join the Crusades; while they
were still further augmented by extending the clerical privi-
lege to all widows, orphans, and other persons in distress.[2]
These courts had jurisdiction over all spiritual causes, but the
phrase is indefinite, and easily covered all questions involving
breach of contract, marriage, testaments, perjury, sacrilege,
etc.[3] In their decisions the ecclesiastical judges were gov-
erned by the canon law, composed of the decrees of Councils
and of Popes, and through their sentences the legislative
authority of the papacy was recognized throughout Europe.[4]

Monstrous though the Ordeals and Trial by Combat must
seem to modern eyes, they were the natural outcome of a theocratic society. In an age of barbarity and violence, at a time
when the administration of justice was crude and uncertain, it

---

[1] Cf. Dante, De Monarchia.   [2] Hallam, Middle Ages, II, 17.
[3] Ibid., II, 18.   [4] Ibid., II, 2.

was but natural that ignorant and superstitious men, implicitly believing in miracles, should endeavor to turn to the infallible judge of all.[1] The ordeals were solemn appeals to the judgment of the Almighty, and, as such, were simply crude, barbarous, but consistent attempts to realize in action the theory of their age.

Finally, all rights rested directly on religion. Those who were outside the pale of the Church possessed no rights. Treaties with infidels were condemned. Fulk, Archbishop of Rheims, declared that there was no difference between becoming the ally of pagans and abandoning the worship of God for the worship of idols.[2] The heretic was outside the Church and beyond the protection of the law. The Council of Constance, in the case of John Huss, even went so far as to declare that an obstinate heretic was unworthy of any privileges, and that no law, human or divine, required men to observe faith with such an one.[3] The case of the Jews differs somewhat from that of the heretic. They were allowed to practise openly, and under the full protection of the law, trades unlawful for Christians. But apparently it was only that the revenue of the government might not be impaired. One of the most lucrative resources of a mediaeval monarch was extortion from the Jews. To use the expressive figure of Hallam, "the kings employed them as sponges to suck up their subjects' money, which they might afterwards express without incurring the odium of direct taxation."[4] If Christians were compelled to keep faith with Jews, it was evidently for the benefit of the Exchequer, and not from any abstract principles of right and justice.

Meanwhile the bounds of the State had been widened. In antiquity woman was outside the limits of the State, while the child was beyond the pale of society. The first great service

---

[1] Hallam, Middle Ages, I, 189. [2] *Ibid.*
[3] Middle Ages, I, 157. [4] *Ibid.*

of Christianity was that it gave to women and children a definite status in society. The fall of the clan system had left them
in a most anomalous position. They were not *sui juris;* they
were not members of the State; and the State was loath to
interfere on their behalf. Christianity supplied what was
wanting.

In the case of the infant its influence was immediately visible.[1] The ancient world recognized no rights of an infant. It
was not a member of society. The father could adopt it, or,
if he chose, with the consent of the five nearest relatives, he
might put it to death. It was not considered a very serious
thing to destroy an insignificant new-born babe, whose suffer-
ings were but slight, and which had as yet formed no social
ties. The most trivial excuses were accepted as sufficient.
In the corrupt days of the Empire abortion, infanticide, and
exposure prevailed to an alarming extent. No particular ob-
loquy attached to these practices. A few moralists might
condemn them, but there were either no penalties attached
to their perpetration, or, if the penalties existed, they were
rarely enforced. Christianity instantly and resolutely denounced them. Infanticide and abortion were not merely
venial homicides; they were murders of the most revolting
type. All the terrors of the Church were employed to suppress
them. The abortionist not only destroyed a life; he doomed
a soul, and no penance, however severe, could quite efface his
guilt. By every means in its power the Church strove to produce a higher sense of the sanctity of human life. Its efforts
were successful, and ever since, the infant has been as definitely
a member of the State as the wealthiest and most powerful
citizen.

The influence of the Church was different in the case of
women. Woman had no proper place in the ancient religions.[2]
The pagan ideal was essentially masculine. Christianity em-

---

[1] Lecky, History of European Morals, II, pp. 17–41.
[2] Hearn, Aryan Household.

phasized the feminine virtues, and insisted upon the moral equality of the sexes. For the first time in the history of humanity it became possible for woman to take her place as the equal of man. But, although Christianity thus proclaimed principles necessary for the permanent advancement of woman, its first effect was unfortunately to lower her condition.[1] Pagan legislation had gradually removed most of the disabilities under which she labored. Under that legislation her personal liberty, and proprietary rights, were greater than they ever were before, or ever have been since.[2] This position was maintained as long as the Roman Law retained its vigor. Unfortunately for civilization, in the struggle between the secular and the ecclesiastical laws, the latter prevailed, and woman fell from her position of equality with man to one of abject inferiority. This was largely due to the spirit of asceticism.[3] The Church by regarding celibacy as the perfect state, and marriage as simply the least objectionable deviation from it, introduced into all the holiest relations of domestic life an element of debasing sensualism. Woman was the temptress luring man from perfection. Concupiscence was the original sin. Through woman sin entered into the world, and she was, in the eyes of the patristic writers, an inferior being, who, in the language of Lecky, ought to be ashamed that she was woman. The necessary reaction from this unnatural and degrading position resulted in that improvement in the status of woman which everywhere accompanied, and was almost the vital principle of, the institution of chivalry. But the chivalric conception of woman, while lofty and elevating, was largely idealistic, and it is only in recent years that women have, in any material degree, recovered the social and civil liberties and rights lost in the decadence of the Roman Law.

With Plato and Aristotle, the strict conception of Justice was confined to the relations of citizens. Between the citizen

---

[1] Lecky, History of European Morals. [2] Maine, Ancient Law.
[3] Lecky, History of European Morals, II, p. 337.

and the alien, Justice could only be spoken of metaphorically.[1]
But the growth of commerce, the triumphs of Alexander, and
the decay of Grecian civil life, tended to produce a more cosmopolitan spirit.   That spirit found expression in the Stoical
philosophy.   The Stoics emphasizing the existence of a rational
order, or law, in the universe, and holding morality to consist
in a life in conformity with that law, taught that all duties to
others, and the State itself, are the products of man's social or
political nature.   Further, they were unable to see in human
nature any justification for the separation of mankind into hostile communities.   They believed that all mankind should constitute one vast commonwealth, in which perfect equality
should prevail.   For the first time, the brotherhood and natural equality of men were distinctly enunciated.   Thus, Stoicism was the expression of that Hellenic cosmopolitanism
which, through the medium of the Roman Law, was to influence the whole future course of civilization.

In a cosmopolitan age, the sympathies of men are, of necessity, projected beyond the narrow bounds of a religious community.   Social unity must then depend upon some other
basis than religious unity.   To that extent, the spirit of universalism has a tendency to weaken the religious feelings of
men.   The growth of classic atheism and scepticism was
simultaneous with the growth of cosmopolitanism.   But there
were many causes operating to preserve the religious foundation of the State, and to prevent the complete rationalization
of society.   In the first place, the universalism of the age was
an abstract one,[2] a philosophic conception, chiefly confined to
one class, with whom it was largely a matter of words.   In the
same way classic scepticism was almost completely limited to
the cultured classes ; the mass of the people continued devout
believers in, or, at least, regular attendants on, the national
and local religious rites ; while even the atheistical regarded

---

[1] Nic. Ethics, V, 6, 4.
[2] Uhlhorn, Conflict of Christianity with Heathenism, bk. I, chap. I, § 1.

those rites as useful to the State, and expedient for the commonalty.[1] But especially powerful in this direction was the deification of the Caesars, which, by the creation of a great imperial cult, embracing all the people of the Empire, and in the formal observances of which every citizen, learned and ignorant alike, might join, was amply sufficient for all the needs of the age. It supplied, side by side with the greatest diversity of local cults, a species of religious unity for the entire civilized world, and the Jews, the only people who refused adhesion to it, were also the only people who remained a perfectly separate and distinct race, hated and hating, viewed with suspicion and distrust, and visited with violent persecutions whenever they openly refused conformity to the edicts of the Emperors.

The era of the Renaissance was also an age of cosmopolitanism. Among the many causes which contributed to bind the European peoples in a closer union, may be enumerated a common origin ; similar languages, especially the common Latin tongue of the clergy and the literati everywhere ; the long religious union under the authority of the Papacy ; the growth of international trade, and the increased refinement of manners and character due to a higher culture, greater intercourse, the institution of chivalry, and a religion of peace. The intellectual activity which always accompanies a period of sudden growth, permeated all classes, and turned with special force to the investigation of theological questions. The schism of the

---

[1] Uhlhorn, Conflict of Christianity with Heathenism, bk. I, chap. I, § 2; Lecky, History of European Morals, vol. I, p. 167: "The atheistic enthusiasm of Lucretius, and the sceptical enthusiasm of some of the disciples of Carneades, were isolated phenomena, and the great majority of ancient philosophers, while speculating with the utmost freedom in private, or in writings that were only read by the few, countenanced, practiced, and even defended the religious rites that they despised. . . . Varro openly professed that there are religious truths which it is expedient that the people should not know, and falsehoods which they should believe to be true. The Academic Cicero and the Epicurean Caesar were both high officers of religion. The Stoics taught that every man should duly perform the religious ceremonies of his country."

Reformation divided Europe into hostile camps ; nation was separated from nation, town from town, brother from brother, on points of religious belief ; the religious unity of Christendom was destroyed ; but the spirit of universalism, no longer a mere abstract sentiment, was too firmly established to be easily extinguished. For a time, indeed, chaos reigned ; all sense of moral responsibility seemed to vanish from public affairs ; the speculative opinions of Machiavelli found their counterpart in the daily practices of statesmen ; but, little by little, men were compelled to recognize that they are united by other bonds than religion alone, that it is possible for them to associate together even when sundered by matters of belief, while the granting of religious toleration showed that States may continue to exist even when divided upon questions of faith.

To the Jurists is due the recognition of a rational foundation for all human association. This they found in the revived Roman Law and the Stoic conception of a common humanity and a Law of Nature. Hobbes and Spinoza first elaborated the Law of Nature into a complete social theory. Seeing clearly that natural rights and natural powers are identical, perceiving also that, in primitive ages, a state of war is the normal condition of mankind, and that, in such ages, peace is the exception established by positive convention, they posited, as the original state of the human race, a pre-social period of absolute anarchy, and regarded society as an association of forbearance, originating in a mutual agreement wherein individuals, for the sake of peace, covenanted to abstain from the exercise of certain of their natural rights on condition that others would do likewise. This idea of a social contract was the dominant theory of the last century and was in perfect accord with the rationalistic tendencies of the Age of Enlightenment ; but it is wholly foreign to the scientific attitude of the present century. From the point of view of science, society is not an accidental or artificial thing ; it is not a mere mass of individuals ; it is an organism possessing life, energy, and growth. This conception of society, as an organism, has been extremely useful in checking crude and unwise attempts at reform, but it seems to have already reached the limit of its usefulness ; its services have been negative, and all attempts to push it further, and to obtain from it positive results, have only led to absurdities and ridiculous analogies. After all, society is not an organism in the same sense that an oyster, or even a man, is one ; it is an organism only in the sense that it is a necessary and natural growth, an organism served by subsidiary organisms, apart from which it has no powers whatever ; to say that it thinks, wills, and acts, is absolutely meaningless, except as an expression for the sum of the thoughts, volitions, and actions of its individual members. Society is an organism by analogy, as an intellectual aid to our fuller understanding of its nature ; but idle attempts to determine its head and its hands, its brain and its nervous system, can scarcely be expected to advance our knowledge of social conditions. Before any further advance can be made, some other and higher conception must be reached, some conception more adequate to all social problems, and by the aid of which we can more fully understand the nature of society.[1]

2. THE DEVELOPMENT OF THE INDIVIDUAL.

The social group, whether city, or clan, or family, and not the individual, was the chief object of concern in the ancient

---

[1] Ritchie, Principles of State Interference, p. 49 : "The truth is that society (or the State) is not an organism because we may compare it to a beast or a man ; but because it cannot be understood by the help of any lower, *i.e.*, less complex conceptions than that of organism. In it as in an organism every part is conditioned by the whole. In a mere aggregate or heap the units are prior to the whole ; in an organism the whole is prior to the parts — *i.e.*, they can only be understood in reference to the whole ; but because the conception of an organism is more adequate to society than the conception of an artificial compound, it does not follow that it is fully adequate. We have just seen that a one-sided application of organic growth leads to difficulties as well as the conception of artificial making. These we can only escape by recognizing a truth which includes them both. We must pass from 'organism' to 'consciousness,' from Nature to the spirit of man."

world. A man and his property belonged not to himself, but to his entire kin, both that which was before and that which was to come after. The family did not exist for man, but man for the family. The archaic household, however, was essentially different from the modern family, with its ties of consanguinity, its limited parental authority, and its transient relationships. It was a permanent corporation having an individuality distinct from its members, possessing a sacerdotal purpose, and founded upon a unity of religious belief.[1] Thus constituted, the household had a corporate character, was perpetual, inextinguishable, immortal, and a man's first duty was to provide for its safe continuance ; until he had offspring to succeed him his duty to his ancestors was unfulfilled. The expansion of the household into the clan, and of the clan into the State, did not in any way alter this view of the relative importance of the individual and the group. The group was still of supreme importance.

From this it resulted, as a matter of course, that the principle of the clan was collective liability.[2] The members of the clan were bound together not merely by a common domestic worship, and a community of land ; they were united by a mutual responsibility ; for his kinsman's misdeeds, each man must answer, and for redressing his injuries, must lend assistance.[3] A communism thus close demands, for its completion and preservation, a communism also in the matter of property. In the archaic household all property was owned by the household in common, while the use lay in the hands of the Father to be employed by him as dictated by custom. Since primitive man can neither obtain mental grasp of, nor consciously direct his life according to, great general principles, these customs must have regulated the very smallest details of life, and the action of the individual must have been fettered in every way conceivable. How minute the regulations of a primitive com-

---

[1] Aryan Household, p. 64.   [2] Maine, Ancient Law, p. 126.
[3] *Ibid.*, p. 127.   La Cité Antique.

munism must be, we may gather from examining those in force, in recent times, among such tribes as the Australian aborigines. Among these tribes, the social life is almost entirely communistic ; the scantiness of subsistence and the danger of famine render the regulations as to food especially minute, so that every animal, which a hunter may capture, is divided according to fixed custom based upon kinship.   Thus, to quote an illustration from Letourneau — " If a man has speared a medium-sized fish, the tail-end belongs to him ; the other falls to his wife.   If, on the contrary, a haul of little fish has been taken, six eels for instance, four of which are large and two small, the division is made thus : The man, his wife, and his maternal uncle with his wife have each a right to one of the big eels ; the last reverts to the elder and younger brothers.   Of the two remaining small eels, one is destined for the children of the mother's brother and the other, circumstances permitting, for the fisherman's married daughter and her husband."[1] In such a society, unchanging custom regulates the entire life of the individual from the first moment of his existence to the last.

It was the weakness of the individual and the necessity of mutual aid which drove men into union.   The accumulation of property, even in its most rudimentary forms, removed that pressure.   It may be doubted if the primitive communism was ever absolute.   No matter what degree of equality might exist in a tribe, individuals were permitted to exercise a more or less exclusive right of property in those articles, weapons and utensils, which they themselves had made and which they alone had used.   Whatever a man had manufactured was regarded as depending, in some sort, upon him ; the articles which he formed were his creation, and had received a portion of his being ; during his lifetime he was allowed a somewhat special ownership in them, and when he died they were broken and placed with him in the tomb, so that he might take them

---

[1] Letourneau, Property, Its Origin and Development, p. 32.

with him to the spirit-world and the future existence on which he had entered. When such a conception had been once entertained, all that is essential in the idea of private property was present, and the institution had only to develop and grow in the course of social evolution.

From private ownership of an object made by a man, to the appropriation of other things upon which he had impressed his personality, was but a short step easily taken. The tendency to confound the thing made with its maker, was soon extended so as to include not only the ground which he had cleared, and the crops which he had sown, but also the captives whom he had seized during successful forays, the women carried away, and the prisoners made slaves by him. Slaves formed the first species of property capable of indefinite increase. It was not until heavy labor, such as that of agriculture, had to be performed that slavery developed ; when the tilling of the soil had grown in importance, the labor of women was displaced, or supplemented, by that of slaves. With the introduction of slavery, agriculture became more and more important, and so produced further capital admitting of accumulation and exchange.

" The establishment of aristocracy and hereditary monarchic power has merely crowned this economic evolution, whereof the point of departure was slavery and the consequent development of agriculture, whence arose the rupture of primitive equality, creation of exchangeable values, development of private property, contrast between rich and poor, foundation of castes, and hereditary succession." [1]

If we now return to the archaic household, it is possible briefly to indicate the transition from communism to individualism which directly preceded our own civilization. The corporate household was monarchic in principle. Over the living the Father ruled with an absolute sway. His was the power

---

[1] Letourneau, Property, Its Origin and Development, p. 61.

of life and death for all who were in his hand, but his government was not one of irresponsible caprice. His power was
bounded by custom and he was responsible for all his acts to
the House Spirits, whose representative on earth he was.[1]
There are no gradations in the power of an absolute monarch.
The members of the ancient household may be divided into
many classes, mother, sons, daughters, slaves, dependents.
But although the circumstances of the individuals varied with
their classes, there were no differences in their rights; strictly
speaking they had no rights; they were all alike in the hand
of the House Father. The son, indeed, may be said to have
had a right of succession, but that was all ; during the lifetime
of his father he was as much a dependent as any slave.[2] The
position of women, whether as wives or daughters, afforded not
even this prospect of ultimate liberty.[3] Manes worship was a
worship of males by males. Woman was, therefore, incapable
of offering the needful sacrifices and so, of necessity, remained
in a subject condition. Prior to marriage, she was in the hand
of her father; after marriage, she served her husband's gods
and passed into his power or that of his father, if living.
Further, the proprietary rights of the household were vested
in the Father. Over all the movables, the herds, the produce
of the lands and the labor of his dependents, his power was
absolute ; but the land itself was inalienable, of it the Father
had only the use, and on it rested, as a first charge, the burden
of maintaining the sacred hearth and the not less sacred tomb.[4]

This corporate family, after slowly decaying for a thousand
years, was finally destroyed by Christianity. During that long
period it had undergone many alterations. The Father's
power had been both increased and diminished. By the time
of the Twelve Tables, it was possible for the *paterfamilias* to
sell the originally inalienable land of the household. By
public law, he was enabled to make a testamentary distribution

---

[1] Aryan Household, p. 95.   [2] *Ibid.*, p. 91.
[3] *Ibid.*, p. 95.   [4] *Ibid.*, p. 74.

of his property, and by the time of Antoninus Pius, the remedy
for his debts lay, not against his person,. but against his family
possessions.   But, in proportion as his proprietary rights increased, his *potestas* diminished.   The corporate family, with
the *patria potestas*, existing as an *imperium in imperio*, was
incompatible with the full development of political authority.
The rights of a father over his son and the rights of the State
over its citizen, while sometimes conflicting, were at all times
antagonistic.   The progress of the State involved the decay of
the paternal power in the family.   Under the religious marriage
with *manus*, the relation of husband and wife was only a particular application of the law of parent and child.   The wife
was not *sui juris*, but was in absolute subjection to her husband.   The introduction of free marriages greatly changed the
position of woman.   She was no longer *materfamilias;* she
was only *uxor;* but what she lost in dignity, she gained in
liberty.   She was now an equal partner with her husband.
Whatever proprietary rights were hers before marriage, remained to her after it.   She was on an equal footing with her
husband both as to her capacity for acquiring, and for dealing
with, her individual property.   Her power over it was not
limited by any marital restrictions.   The power of the father
over his sons and dependents was jealously watched, and
gradually restricted by the State.   Originally, the father had
an absolute control over both the person and the possessions
of his son.   By the time of Augustus, an exception was made
in favor of the *peculium castrense* of the *filiusfamilias miles*,
an exception which, after the reign of Diocletian, was extended
to the official remuneration of all sons in public offices ; while
by the enactments of various Emperors, the power of life and
death over sons and slaves was greatly reduced, if not altogether destroyed.

But it was reserved for Christianity to deal the final blow.
The religion of the hearth, and not natural affection, was the
bond of union in the household.   To that religion Christianity
was, of necessity, hostile.   As an uncompromising monotheism,

it forbade, alike, the worship of the gods of the Pantheon and the service of departed ancestors. Wherever the early missionaries made converts, the family religion, with its domestic altar and household priests disappeared, and its place was filled by those ties of natural affection which, in the progress of ages, had grown sufficiently strong for the purpose. It was not necessary for this result that the head of the household should become a Christian. Antiquity could not conceive of a woman having any gods other than those of her husband. Christianity asserted the right and duty of every woman to make choice for herself. The majority of the early converts were women. Families were divided, and the worship of the Lars became impossible. No man could make any acceptable offering to the gods when the sacred fire of the hearth was tended by a wife of alien faith. When the inroads of the barbarians again introduced the corporate family into Europe, it was only for it to share the fate of its classical predecessor. Christian priests were the advisers of the kings, and manes worship was not more hostile to the spiritual requirements of the Church, than was a community of property to its temporal interests.

Christianity, however, did more for the advancement of the individual than merely destroy the last shreds of the corporate family. As already noticed, Christianity, besides asserting the religious liberty of the individual and the moral equality of the sexes, laid great stress on the importance of human life and employed it in the protection of the infant. But this was only part of a greater whole. The Church elevated the conception of the value of human life, but it was of the life of the individual, not of the social atom, — of the man, not of the citizen. For antiquity, religion was a matter affecting men chiefly as parts of a social order, as members of a family, a city, or a State. Christianity appealed to the individual as an individual. Antiquity was without that sense of sin and of the need of salvation which was introduced by the Christian religion. The individual man now became of supreme worth. Human beings were now more than members of an earthly social system ; had a destiny higher and more enduring than could be supplied by any temporal existence ; they were immortal souls, destined to an eternity of bliss or woe, an eternity depending entirely upon personal choice and individual development. The State was no longer the all in all for men. The complete development of man was no longer possible through the agency of society. Men had caught a glimpse of another order, of another life into which each must enter alone, not as a member of a certain family, or according to the State to which he had belonged, but upon the basis of his own personality and of what he had done with it. The new religion forced upon men a new sense of responsibility for individual development. Primitive solidarity and altruism were rendered forever impossible by the Christian doctrine of the sinfulness of man and the need of a personal salvation. The tremendous force given to the conception of sin by the early Fathers of the Church accelerated this tendency. Its effect was immediately seen in the solitary ascetic life led by the hermits of the desert, probably the most extreme individualism ever attempted or attained by men. The monastic orders continued the same movement, being founded upon the abandonment of all political and social ties. From the triumph of Christianity dates the triumph of the individual. From that moment the welfare of the individual for this life, as well as for the next, became the chief object of solicitude. Man no longer lived for society but society existed for man.

But while individualism was thus rapidly advancing in one direction, in the realm of thought it entirely disappeared.[1] Under the influence of the Greek philosophy, the minds of the learned had been largely emancipated from all the restraints imposed by any belief in the supernatural. Liberty of thought had advanced with mighty leaps. Upon the establishment of the Imperial power, the reactionary policy and tyranny of

---

[1] Holland, Rise of Intellectual Liberty.

Augustus and his immediate successors, suddenly reinforced as it was by Christianity, checked this progress. The subjection of citizen to sovereign, and of reason to faith, was insured by the organization of the Christian hierarchy. The spread of Christianity, the repressive influence of Imperial power, and the steady increase of poverty, all resulted in the production of an intellectual lethargy, fatal to mental liberty and activity, the extinction of which was rendered complete by the inroads of the barbarians. From that moment originality of thought, the natural product of free personality, disappeared for ages and faith in authority supplied the place of rational conviction.

It was not till the thirteenth century that the minds of men began to awaken. Through the long Middle Ages man had slumbered under "the spell of race," but with the dawn of the fourteenth century that spell was broken and the dogmatic slumberers began to awaken to a new sense of personality.[1] This was the result of that spirit of Cosmopolitanism which was rationalizing society. This spirit, which is itself an extremely advanced condition of individualism, was due largely to the revival of learning, which by providing men with a multitude of new sources of purely intellectual satisfaction independent of time and place, undermined the narrow and intense patriotism of the Italian citizen for his city, and enabled the exile to feel at home everywhere. At the same time, the rapid growth of commerce drew all lands closer together, while the great increase of wealth and culture produced new wants and supplied the means of satisfying them. The restlessness incident to an era when new regions are being discovered, fostered a restlessness of spirit which soon found old surroundings and old customs irksome. Men began to throw off the fetters of custom, the greatest limitation on the development of personality; they demanded liberty to mould their own lives free from the restrictions of the past. Aroused to a new consciousness of the supreme worth of the individual, each demanded

---

[1] Burckhardt, Renaissance in Italy.

the freedom of self-development, the unfettered growth of personality, by expansion from within as distinguished from the imposition of form from without through the moulding influences of external authority. The men of the Renaissance strove for the harmonious development of both the spiritual and material existences so that the fifteenth century is, above all, the era of the many-sided man.

Christianity awakened men to a sense of personal responsibility and of the value of the individual. So long as this remained divorced from, and hostile to, intellectual liberty it perforce remained largely inoperative. But when under the stimulus of the Renaissance it was joined to intellectual activity, perfect individuality followed ; the Reformation laid the foundations of religious liberty ; the struggles of the seventeenth and eighteenth centuries resulted in the establishment of political freedom ; while the French Revolution, by assimilating real property to personal, and freeing both of almost all legal duties, carried individualism to the verge of anarchy. To-day we are confronted, on the one hand, by a philosophic attempt to reach a more complete individualism as the basis of the perfect State, and, on the other hand, by a practical Socialist reaction towards an increased social solidarity.

CHAPTER II.

THE idea of equality enters in some sort into every conception of Justice. This has been so in all ages, even the most primitive. The majority of men cherish the belief that the equal is the just, as a mere hazy, undefined notion. For some it is simply an equality before the law; for others it is a fixed ratio between reward and desert; many regard it as including an equality of political power; while others would extend it to all social relations. That the equal is the just is a truism universally acknowledged. Thus the Roman jurists, ignoring the distinction between law and morality, speak of *jus*, the *justi atque injusti scientia* as *ars boni et aequi*. Plato declared that equality of the higher kind is the judgment of Zeus and the true principle of justice. Aristotle elaborated that idea, and from it constructed the most influential of all his theories. Pascal seems to have believed that justice demands an equality of goods,[1] and John Stuart Mill claimed that equality is universally regarded as the ideal of justice, and that men deviate from it only from motives of expediency. But when men come to define what they regard this equality as being, they differ widely, all the more widely because a purely abstract conception of Justice is almost meaningless, and every conception not thus abstract is inextricably entangled with all manner of political, social, religious, and industrial problems. Yet, broadly speaking, however much individuals may differ in matters of detail, in the main issue they may be separated into only two schools, according as they adopt one or the other of the two principal meanings of the word equality, first as implying the same magnitude or degree, and second as indicating uniform proportion.

---

[1] Thoughts, VII, 7.

The second of these classes finds its earliest exponents in
Plato and Aristotle.   In *The Republic*, and indeed throughout
all his works, Plato attends almost exclusively to that phase of
Justice which his great successor called Distributive.   In his
treatment of this he is really at one with Aristotle.   Aristotle
definitely expresses what Plato says indefinitely.   Both believe
inequality to be a fact of nature, and therefore just.[1]   Both regard this natural unequalness as the basis of all true class distinctions.   Both think fitness to be the standard which should
measure the distribution of goods,[2] and both hold that that
distribution should be made in a geometrical ratio.   Thus Plato
says, "The old saying that equality makes friendships, is happy
and true, but there is obscurity and confusion as to what sort
of equality is meant.   For there are two equalities which are
called by the same name, but are in many ways almost the
opposite of one another.   One of them may be introduced without difficulty by any State or any legislator in the distribution
of honors; this is the rule of measure, weight, and number
which apportions them.   But there is another equality of a
better and a higher kind which is not so easily recognized.
This is the judgment of Zeus; among men it avails but little;
that little is, however, the source of the greatest good to cities
and to individuals.   For it gives to the greater more, and to
the inferior less, and in proportion to the nature of each, above
all, greater honor always to the greater virtue, and to the less
less, and to either in proportion to their respective measure
of virtue and education.   And this is Justice, and is ever the
true principle of States at which we ought to aim, and, according to this, order the city."[3]   And this is nothing but what
Aristotle states more tersely when he says: "And there must
be the same equality between the persons and the things; as
the things are to one another so must the persons be.   For if

---

[1] Republic, III, 415.   Politics, 1. 5.
[2] Republic, IV, 423.   Nic. Ethics, V. 3. 7.
[3] Laws, VI, 757.

the persons be not equal their shares will not be equal; and this is the source of endless disputes and accusations, when persons who are equal do not receive equal shares, or when persons who are not equal receive equal shares."[1] Aristotle was, however, in advance of Plato, inasmuch as he saw that it is impossible to obtain any absolute standard by which to determine this distribution.[2] He clearly perceived that one virtue cannot be quantitatively compared with another, or moral qualities with intellectual or with material possessions, or the qualities of one man with those of another. The standard must be purely subjective.

The Aristotelian conception of Distributive Justice, as a geometrical ratio between the quantities of goods distributed and the qualities of the persons receiving, has been the dominant theory of Justice ever since, and, in some one form or other, has been accepted by the majority of people from his time to the present day. It is the idea of Justice involved in the definition of the Roman Law: Justice is the constant and perpetual wish to render every one his due.[3] It is likewise the theory elaborated with details essentially his own by Leibnitz,[4] and it is the one which is held by Schmoller to exhibit the true ideal of Justice in the economic sphere.[5] It is, in short, the ideal of Justice of which the existing social conditions are but an imperfect realization.

In his many different works Plato's treatment of Justice is not always by any means uniform or consistent. This may be due in part to the development and change of his ideas in process of time, but it is more especially the result of changes in the standpoint from which he viewed his subject. In *The Laws*, from which the preceding extract is taken, Plato was

---

[1] Nic. Ethics, V. 3. 6.   [2] Politics, III, 9.
[3] Institutes of Justinian, I, 1.
[4] Leibnitz, Preface of the Codex Diplomaticus Juris Gentium.
[5] Gustav Schmoller, Idea of Justice in Political Economy.

engaged in deducing the true principles of, and the best institutions for existing society; on the other hand, in the earlier work, *The Republic*, he endeavored to depict an ideal but impossible State ; and so many things regarded as just in one dialogue are held to be unjust in the other. Thus, for example, in *The Republic* the administration of justice is to be the work of a single class of the citzens; in the later work this is denounced as unjust, and it is proclaimed that every citizen, no matter to what class he may belong, should equally participate in the deciding of suits, whether public or private, and yet the guardian class exists in both dialogues.[1]

The philosopher who, when attempting to discover the ideal of justice which is embodied, however imperfectly, in society, begins with the consideration of the powers and claims of individuals, must arrive at a concept of Justice essentially different from that to which he would have attained had the point of his departure been the nature of the State, its functions, its needs, and the best means of its development. In Plato we find the two ideals which are reached from these opposing extremes. When we consider, first of all, the powers, the responsibilities, and the destiny of man, as man and not as the social atom, we are compelled to admit that the individual is above society. When we think of the nature of personality, involving as it does powers of expansive growth and of self-determination, liberty (*i.e.*, originality, spontaneity, or the development of the man from within, as opposed to the imposition of form from without) assumes almost the character of a sacred right, and the possession of superior intelligence, or superior virtue, or even of superior physical force, is seen to carry with it greater responsibility and to constitute, in itself, a claim to commensurate reward. The unfettered development of personality demands the right of man to take in proportion to his various powers. This is the concept of Justice contained in the quotation from *The Laws* given above ; very different is the ideal of

---

[1] Laws, VI, 768.

Justice found in *The Republic* and reached by an analysis of the perfect State.

Looking at society as something more than a collection of human units, as a grand whole, an organism possessing an individuality and a life of its own, as the necessary condition of the preservation and advancement of the race, and as indispensable even to the happiness of the individual, society rises superior to its individual members, and the interests of the whole become more important than the happiness of any single person or group of persons. In *The Republic*, Plato approaches the subject from this standpoint, and arrives at a conception of justice which, deprived of all its purely local details, is essentially the ideal reached by every student who has thus begun his investigation. Differences in the powers of individuals do not, under this view, constitute any claim to diversity of rewards or inequality of happiness. Such differences are only means to an end ; they do not exist for the benefit of the individual, but for the use of the State ; and the perfect State will not simply take men in the positions in which it finds them, but it will place men in those positions for which Nature has fitted them, and in which they will serve with benefit to the State rather than with profit to themselves. Plato therefore divides the inhabitants of his city into three classes, guardians, auxiliaries, and traders. To the guardians, as the intellect of the commonwealth, belongs the task of ruling the city and guiding its energies ; to the auxiliaries is allotted the task of defending the State from its enemies ; and to the trader belongs the duty of providing for its material wants. The principle upon which the citizens are assigned to the different classes is fitness. Each man and each woman is placed in the position which he or she is qualified to fill. Birth alone does not place a citizen in any class. Each individual is to be put to the use for which nature designed him, and it is the duty of the guardians to degrade their own offspring when inferior, and to elevate into the rank of guardians the children of the lower classes when naturally superior. To each class, and to each individual in the class, particular duties are to be assigned, and the principle of justice, expressed in an outward form, is, that every man shall do his own work.   It is just that each man should have and do what is his own.   Although but little damage would result from a cobbler doing the work of a carpenter, yet if such an one attempted to become a warrior, or a warrior a guardian, great harm to the State would follow, and injury to the State is the greatest evil, doing which is injustice.   Thus the meddling of one class with the duties of another is injustice, while, on the other hand, Justice is when the trader, the auxiliary, and the guardian are content each to do the work assigned to them, and for which they are qualified by nature.

But while Plato thus recognizes the existence of natural inequalities among men and makes use of those inequalities for the service of the State, he does not regard them as constituting any claim to inequality of happiness.   The classes to whom the power of the State is entrusted are not permitted to reap from that power material advantages for themselves and their friends.   Communism is the keystone of *The Republic*. The destruction of the family, with its separate interests and its individual property, and the substitution for it of a community of wives, of children, and of goods, is the fitting completion of his ideal social structure.   The guardian is merely a ruling pauper ; he can never know the joys of ownership, or the power of wealth ; he can never taste of the luxuries and comforts of life ; his is the arduous career of the warrior, without its counterbalancing pleasures.   To Adimantus, who urges that in this he is destroying the happiness of men, Plato answers that no individual has a vested right to happiness. The principle of happiness resides in the State as a whole, and the aim of the legislator should not be the disproportionate happiness of any one class, but the happiness of the entire body-politic.   That happiness depends upon the harmony and order prevailing in the State, and, if it is to be realized, the several classes must be compelled each to perform its appointed duties, and thus the State will grow up in a noble unity and the different orders of citizens will receive the proportion of happiness which nature assigns them. The only inequality of pleasures permitted to exist in *The Republic* is that arising naturally from the division of duties. To each class certain duties belong, and to the performance of those duties certain pleasures pertain, while certain other pleasures are of necessity contrary to them. Since it is wrong for the individuals of one class to usurp the duties of another, they ought never to expect to enjoy their peculiar pleasures. The guardians can only look for such pleasures as naturally accompany the performance of their duties, and if, therefore, they make the pleasures of revelling boors their ideal of happiness, they will be justly disappointed. Plato, with an Athenian citizen's contempt for commerce and manual labor, admitted inequalities in the honor allotted to the different divisions of society. This exception, to the Greek mind a very real one, is the only exception of *The Republic*. Otherwise the conception of Justice involved in the Platonic socialism is the conception contained in all communistic theories. Ideal Justice demands the absolute equality of all social conditions.

The idea that all men are, or ought to be, absolutely equal, is one of comparatively late growth.[1] It was unknown in the earlier ages of political development, and is not found at the cradle of the race. The earliest form of political society was the theocracy, a form of government hostile alike to liberty and to equality. This hostility finds expression in the institution of castes. Society divides naturally into a series of social strata. It is arranged in a divinely appointed order, and it would be more than folly, it would be gross impiety, for one of low caste to imagine himself as the equal of a man of superior rank. The priest and the king are human divinities, the representatives of God on earth, and as such there can be no ques-

---

[1] Upon this section see May, Democracy in Europe ; Laurent, L'Histoire de l'Humanité, tome XVII ; La Liberté et l'Égalité.

tion of equality with them.   The sacerdotal caste rules ; inferior castes obey.   The inequality is absolute, and extends even
to the criminal law ; what is permissible from the Brahmin to
the Sudra, is a deadly crime from the Sudra to the Brahmin,
and the severity of the division is only mitigated by a vague
hope of a posthumous equality in another stage of existence.
All theocracies, however, are not uniformly unequal.   Thus
Buddha, in proclaiming the religious equality, undermined the
caste system, and made a civic and political equality possible.
The Jewish theocracy also was unfavorable to caste, while its
laws seem to have been especially designed to preserve a social
equality.   The limitation of the priesthood to a single tribe
was, in effect, the creation of a caste, but the Jewish conception of the priest, as "man's representative before God, not
God's representative before men," prevented that caste obtaining a divine power.

In Greece the theocracy was short-lived.   The Zeus-born
hero never ruled in independence.   At every step he was
obliged to obtain the consent of his nobles and people assem-
bled in the agora.   When at the very threshold of the historic
period he disappeared, the assembly of the agora remained,
the central political institution of oligarchic or democratic
republics.   There was, however, no theoretical equality in
even the most democratic of these republics, Athens, during
the heyday of its political activity.   Theirs was an equality of
citizens, not of men.   Labor was degrading to a free man.
The working classes, metics and slaves, who formed the great
majority of the population, were inferior races evidently designed by nature for a subject condition.   Even between citizens the claims of noble birth were freely recognized in the
popular leaders.   With the decay of Grecian civil life, a
change began to make itself felt.   In its last days the Athenian democracy was verging on communism.   The free distribution of corn and money, the theorica, and the payment of
the citizens for attending public meetings, were all communistic measures.   The idea of a natural equality was arising.

Aristotle admits that there were in Athens, in his day, men who denied that slavery was according to the law of nature, and Athens had scarcely fallen under the yoke of Philip, when Zeno, the Stoic, proclaimed that all men are by nature equal.

Stoicism, by founding on the unity of the race and the brotherhood of man, and laying stress on the dignity of human nature, tended towards a doctrine of equality. Thus slavery ceased to be the sign of an essential inferiority. It came to be regarded as an accident, in no way affecting the real dignity of men. The slave might be free in virtue, while the master was a slave to vice.[1] The institution was recognized as contrary to the law of nature, but it was not on that account abolished. Stoicism was a system of morality too lofty, and requiring too great strength of character, to influence directly the mass of the people.[2] It was powerless to effect fundamental changes in their domestic institutions. Stoicism accomplished much through the medium of the Roman Law, but its influence over the law has been much overestimated. It has been said that the transformation of the Roman Law from the narrow law of the city to the law of the world, was chiefly the work of Stoicism.[3] Roman conservatism and reverence for law, however, rendered impossible any changes either sudden, or for the sake of mere abstract principles.[4] Stoicism had no place in the establishment of the *jus gentium* or in the praetorian edicts. It did influence the scientific jurists, but even there its influence was confined to the form, it had no power to determine the matter, of the law. Roman law always proceeded from the concrete example to the underlying principle;[5] Stoicism only decided the form in which the principles so deduced

---

[1] Lecky, Hist. of Eur. Morals, vol. I, 306.   [2] *Ibid.*, vol. I, 194.

[3] "A third and still more important service which Stoicism rendered to popular morals was in the formation of Roman Jurisprudence." Lecky, Hist. of Eur. Morals, Vol. I, 294. Denis, Theories et Idees morales dans l'Antiquite, vol. II, p. 214.

[4] Sohm, Institutes of Roman Law.   [5] *Ibid.*

should be expressed. So the Roman jurist, while acknowledging that all men are by nature born free and equal,[1] did not therefore endeavor to abolish slavery. He contented himself with mitigating the hardships of the institution, and saved the consistency of his system by regarding the slave as *res*, not *persona*.[2] Through the Roman Law, Stoicism did confer one lasting benefit on humanity, by providing the jurists with those maxims of equity and equality with which they prefaced their system, and which have ever since been the fundamental principles of judicial interpretation.[3]

The doctrine of equality was greatly strengthened by the advent of Christianity. Like Buddhism, Christianity proclaimed a religious equality. The teachings of Christ, texts like, "If thou wilt be perfect go and sell that thou hast and give to the poor ";[4] "He that is greatest among you let him be as the younger, and he that is chief as he that doth serve,"[5] and the communistic practices of the early Church, were all favorable to the growth of a belief in the natural equality of men, and in later ages formed most potent arguments in its support.

But the Church soon departed from its primitive simplicity. The conversion of the Empire placed the ecclesiastical authority on the side of the civil power, and the numerous texts commanding subjection to authority acquired great force. The Church remained true to its ideal of religious equality, and in morality recognized no difference between the noble and the slave, but it never meddled with the established civic and political order. Such aspirations after equality as remained, found expression in the monastic life, with its vows of poverty, as something apart from the natural order of the world. The Church also abandoned its original constitution in favor of an elaborate hierarchical system, but even here an important

---

[1] Ulpian, Digest, lib. 1, tit. 1-4.
[2] On this fiction of law see Lorimer, Institutes of Law, pp. 154-7.
[3] Lecky, Hist. of Eur. Morals.
[4] Matthew xix, 21.   [5] Luke xxii, 26.

practical equality was maintained; the son of the meanest peasant on entering the Church was eligible for any office; could rise to be a bishop, the peer of the proudest nobles; might fill the highest offices of the State; might become a cardinal, the equal of secular princes; or even ascend the throne of St. Peter as the master of the world. The Feudal System, the secular complement of the ecclesiastical hierarchy, also contained germs of equality. Slavery gave place to serfdom. The personal dependent, the legal *thing*, was succeeded by the man attached to the soil, not free, but still recognized by the law as a man. The allegiance of the subject to his suzerain also differed materially from the allegiance of the ancient citizen to his State. The allegiance of the citizen to the State was absolute; he had no right to oppose the State; his individuality was absorbed in it. Under the Feudal System the oath of allegiance was a contract; the subject swore to serve and obey his lord and in return received certain rights; the obligations were reciprocal.[1] Further, the balance between the estates — kings, nobles, and burghers — was such that while each exercised certain degrees of social and political influence, no single class could establish itself in absolute supremacy.

Nor were instances of political equality entirely lacking during the Middle Ages. Throughout Europe and especially in Italy, there early arose free city republics bearing a wonderful resemblance to those of ancient Greece. In the forests of Switzerland, pure democratic cantons were produced by the pastoral simplicity of a mountain land. But in none of these instances was there any theoretical foundation in a doctrine of natural equality. Still those ideas of liberty and equality, which had been bequeathed to posterity by the thinkers of antiquity, never entirely died out. Within the shadows of the schools most advanced political theories were sometimes

---

[1] "Qu'est-ce, en définitive, que la hiérarchie féodale ? Une association d'hommes ayant des droits et des obligations réciproques. Les obligations et les droits diffèrent d'après les diverses classes, mais il y a un principe commun, le contrat, c'est à dire l'idée du droit." Laurent, l'Histoire de l'Humanité, tome XVIII, 399.

formulated. Thus Thomas Aquinas advocated representative government with a parliament consisting of king, lords, and commons, and held that rebellion is the right of a dissatisfied people. With the revival of learning and the tremendous mental stimulus of the Reformation these ideas received a new vitality. The religious movement, the attempt to return to the simplicity of primitive Christianity, produced as its extreme the communism of the Anabaptists. The philosophic movement gave rise to Sir Thomas More's Utopia, the first attempt to construct an ideal State on the basis of absolute equality. For Plato and Cicero, justice is the rule of the natural superior over the natural inferior ; in the Platonic ideal the State is divided into classes for government, for war, and for labor, and there is no equality of power except between members of the same class. With More the equality is social, industrial, and political ; within the family group the government is patriarchal, descending from the oldest man and his wife to the next oldest couple ; beyond those groups it is by annually elected magistrates and councils ; equal power, equal labor, equal benefit are the keynotes of the Utopia, the first deliverance of modern socialism.

The dictum of Zeno, " All men are by nature equal," was applied by the philosophers only as an ethical principle, a criterion of what ought to be. Even by the jurists it was adopted only as an ethical ideal and not as a basis of existing law. It was reserved for Hobbes to give it supreme power as the actual foundation of all society, and the test of all existing political institutions. Hobbes begins by declaring, as a fact, that all men are, at all times, absolutely equal.[1] The distinctions which have been created by law, are violations of this equality. Equal

---

[1] Leviathan, pt. I, chap. XIII. "Nature has made men so equal in the faculties of the body and mind : as that though there be found one man sometimes manifestly stronger in body, or of quicker mind than another ; yet when all is reckoned together, the difference between man and man is not so considerable, as that one man can claim to himself any benefit to which another may not pretend as well as he."

powers involve equal rights, so that every man has by nature an equal right to everything.[1] From this it follows that the state of nature is a state of war, for equality produces distrust, and distrust war.[2] Anarchic war must be harmful to every one, and under such conditions the lives of men must be low, brutish, and short.[3] Reason teaches every man that if peace is to be established, agreement is necessary, and if he is to obtain quiet possession of one portion of the sum total of human possessions, he must resign all other portions.[4] To carry out this agreement government is necessary, and in order that government may perform its work perfectly, it must be absolute ; men must resign all their rights and powers. Of all forms of government an absolute monarchy, uncontrolled by councils composed either of peers or commons, is the best, for such a government, where one man commands alone and all others equally obey, is the minimum violation of natural equality necessary to secure the desired end, peace and order.[5]

Spinoza agrees with Hobbes in positing an original state of natural equality and the formation of government by a social contract; but he differs from him as to the rights of men under government. Hobbes regards men under government as having surrendered all those rights which had belonged to them in a state of nature. Spinoza, on the other hand, more logically recognizes that powers and rights are not merely identical for the individual; they are also identical for States. Only that government would have the right to be absolute which has the power so to be. For Hobbes, natural right exists only in a state of nature ; the formation of government destroys it. Spinoza is more consistent ; with him natural

---

[1] Philosophic Elements of a Free Citizen, chap. I, § 10.
[2] *Ibid.*, chap. I, § 12. Leviathan, pt. I, chap. XIII.   [3] *Ibid.*
[4] *Ibid.*, pt. I, chap. XIV.
[5] *Ibid.*, pt. II, chap. XXX. " The inequality of subjects proceedeth from the acts of sovereign power : and therefore has no more place in the presence of the sovereign . . . than the inequality between kings and their subjects in the presence of the King of Kings."

right continues; man has still a natural right to do what he can, and the right of a State over its subjects is equal to the excess of its power over the powers of those subjects.[1]

Rousseau made the next great advance in the doctrine of absolute equality. Hobbes and Spinoza posited an original state of equality as a fact, but they were the only men of note who ever ventured so far. Rousseau adopted the conception of a social contract as the basis of an adequate theory of the State; but he would not say that the State had been preceded by a period of anarchy and natural equality. In his opinion the state of nature is something which does not, perhaps never did, and probably never will exist,[2] but it nevertheless constitutes an ideal not less attractive because not real, an ideal towards which all social progress should tend. The state of nature is no longer a repulsive picture of degraded anarchy; in the pages of Rousseau it becomes a fascinating Arcadian idyl, and to him its widespread popularity was due. Civilization, although it has not originated all the inequalities of men, has aggravated the natural inequalities, and to that extent has been a positive injury to mankind. Civilization, as it is, must be destroyed, and the attainment of an absolute equality should constitute the goal of all social progress.

After Rousseau the doctrine of equality spread rapidly. The French Revolution gave it practical interest, and its influence is to be seen in even the most divergent systems of thought. It is to be found in the writings of Bentham, where it is assumed as the principle of division of the greatest happiness for

---

[1] " As regards political theories, the difference which you inquire about between Hobbes and myself, consists in this, that I always preserve natural right intact, and only allot to the chief magistrates in every State a right over their subjects commensurate with the excess of their power over the power of their subjects. This is what always takes place in the state of nature." Spinoza. Correspondence, Letter L.

[2] Discours sur l'Origine et les Fondemens de l'Inégalité parmi les Hommes, Préface. "Un état qui n'existe plus, qui n'a peut-être point existé, qui probablement n'existera jamais, et dont il est pourtant nécessaire d'avoir des notions justes, pour bien juger de notre état présent."

the greatest number; the sum total of happiness will go furthest when it is divided into equal portions, and the division
must accordingly be made on the basis of "every one is to
count for one and nobody for more than one." [1] John Stuart
Mill also regarded equality as an ideal for society, only limited
by questions of expediency. Thus he says, " Each person
maintains that equality is the dictate of justice except where
he thinks that expediency requires inequality." [2] " All persons
are deemed to have a right to equality except when some recognized social expediency requires the reverse, and hence all
social inequalities which have ceased to be considered expedient assume the character, not of simple inexpediency, but of
injustice." [3] Even Kant was affected by the doctrine. In his
case it was the natural effect of an extreme individualist theory
of the State. Each man is more than a mean; he is an end-
in-himself, and as such has a right to demand equal freedom,
the basis of all law. [4]

Admit, with Zeno and Hobbes, that men are, as a matter of
fact, by nature absolutely equal, and there is no conflict between these two ideals of Justice, as under either ideal it is
just that equals should receive equal shares. Admit, on the
other hand, that men are not thus naturally equal, and the two
ideals stand over against one another in sharp antagonism.
The ideal of Individualism, that men should receive in proportion to their powers, that superior intelligence and superior
virtue should receive commensurate reward, involves as a corollary freedom, the liberty of self-development, *i.e.*, free growth
of the personality from within. In order that a man may fully
reap the benefits of his own nature he must be free, his personality must have full scope for spontaneous development.
The Socialistic ideal, on the contrary, has no place for unre-

---

[1] Bentham, Principles of Morals and Legislation.
[2] Utilitarianism, chap. V.   [3] *Ibid.*
[4] Kant, Philosophy of Law.

strained development.   The unchecked growth of unequal personalities means only greater and greater inequalities.   The'
equality of men, not being a fact of nature, must be produced
artificially by the imposition of force, either social or political;
instead of expansion from within there is the imposition of
form from without.   Liberty and equality, though linked together as the watchword of modern revolutionary movements,
are in reality widely separated as the central ideas of two
opposing conceptions of Justice.   Recently Mr. Spencer has
made a determined effort to unite these two extremes, and to
develop a theory which shall have a place at once for freedom
and for equality.

Mr. Spencer recognizes in the fully developed idea of Justice
two terms, a positive and a negative.   Approaching the question
from the standpoint of the scientist and evolutionist philosopher, he is compelled to maintain that man is, and always must
be, as much subject to the law of the survival of the fittest as
are the inferior animals.   That law demands for the preservation of the species "that among adults the individuals best
adapted to the conditions of their existence shall prosper most,
and that individuals least adapted to the conditions of their
existence shall prosper least."[1]   In its ethical aspect, this law
implies that "each individual ought to receive the benefits and
the evils of his own nature and consequent conduct."[2]   This
forms the positive element of our idea of Justice which constantly finds expression in such phrases as "He got no more
than he deserved" and "He fairly earned his reward."   The
formula expresses only a pre-requisite of life in general, and,
if all men led solitary and independent lives, it would contain
all that is essential in the concept of Justice.   But men do not
thus live alone.   Their gregarious instincts and mutual needs
compel them to dwell together in social unions which are more
or less complete.   This presence of others renders it necessary
that individual activities should be mutually restrained.   In

---

[1] Justice, p. 17.   [2] *Ibid.*, p. 13.

society the truth is recognized, "that each individual carrying on the actions which subserve his life, and not prevented from receiving their normal results, good and bad, shall carry on these actions under such restraints as are imposed by the carrying on of kindred actions by other individuals, who have similarly to receive such normal results, good and bad."[1] In society men act in spheres which are limited by the presence and spheres of others. This limitation imposed by association furnishes the negative element of Justice. The formula of Justice which will unite these two elements, the positive which is a pre-requisite of life in general, and the negative, which is the necessary result of many lives being carried on together, is — "Every man is free to do that which he wills, provided he infringes not the equal freedom of any other man."[2] For Mr. Spencer, Justice is "the liberty of each, limited only by the like liberty for all." In this way the apparently opposite elements of Justice, which have produced so many one-sided theories, are reconciled. Equality and inequality are joined together. "The equality concerns the mutually-limited spheres of action which must be maintained if associated men are to coöperate harmoniously. The inequality concerns the results which each may achieve by carrying on his actions within the implied limits. No incongruity exists when the ideas of equality and inequality are applied, the one to the bounds and the other to the benefits. Contrariwise, the two may be, and must be, simultaneously asserted."[3] Here the watchword of Justice is neither liberty nor equality; it is equal freedom. Is this union of liberty and equality an actuality, or even a possibility, or is it only a matter of words, and how far does it meet the needs of those who are groping for a theory of Justice which will satisfy the moral convictions of the race?

---

[1] Justice, p. 21.   [2] *Ibid.*, p. 46.   [3] *Ibid.*, p. 43.

CHAPTER III.

LIBERTY is a shibboleth of wondrous power in the mouths ·of that class of political philosophers of which Mr. Herbert Spencer is the recognized leader. Its complete realization, in the form of absence of restraint, is for them the goal of all progress.

"What is the rule whereby the majority is to guide itself as to when it should interfere with the freedom of individuals and when it should not? It is this : while according the same worship to liberty in politics that we accord to honesty in private dealings, hardly permitting ourselves to believe that its violation can in any case be wise or permanently expedient, while leaning to liberty as we lean to truth and deviating from it only when the arguments in favor of despotism are absolutely overwhelming, our aim should be to find out by study of history what those classes of acts are in which State interference shows signs of becoming weakened, and, so far as possible, to hasten on the day of complete freedom in such matters." [1]

For writers of this class, the power of the State and the freedom of the individual stand over against each other in sharp antagonism. Whatever adds to the one subtracts from the other ; increased State activity involves decreased freedom for the individual ; while increase of liberty can only result from a weakening of State interference. Error must result from such a position, not merely because of its unscientific arithmetical conception of the relation of the Individual to the State,[2] but also because it leaves entirely out of account a third most important factor, an intermediate organization, society. The State and society are not identical and must not be confounded. Commonplace as the distinction between

---

[1] Donisthorpe, Limits of Liberty, p. 78.
[2] Ritchie, Principles of State Interference.

them is, it must be insisted upon since it is constantly ignored by writers upon all sides. It is not only overlooked by many who, in the name of Liberty, demand the lessening of the powers of the State ; it is also ignored by multitudes who demand their increase in the name of Humanity. These latter but too often oppose millions of isolated individuals, incapable of voluntary coöperation, on the one hand, to the State, as the only known medium of combination and cohesion, on the other. Theories which begin by failing to distinguish between Society and the State must inevitably end in false conclusions.

The *Century Dictionary* defines society as " Those persons collectively who are united by the common bond of neighborhood and intercourse, and who recognize one another as associates, friends, and acquaintances." The same authority quotes as approved Woolsey's definition of the State as "a community of persons living within certain limits of territory under a permanent organization which aims to secure the prevalence of justice by self-imposed law." [1] On the one hand we see multitudinous associations and combinations, vague and indefinite, varied and flexible, ever changing, circle within circle, linked together in countless ways and without assignable bounds ; on the other, definite organization, rigid and permanent, with fixed territorial limits, and guided by law. As stating this contrast, Marcus Aurelius could say with truth, " So far as I am an Antonine my country is Rome ; so far as I am a man, it is the world." [2]

It is customary with many to oppose society, as the free spontaneous combination of men, to the State, as an apparatus of force and coercion. Thus Beaulieu, " Side by side with the political organization of collective forces proceeding by way of injunction and restraint, that is the State, there arise on all sides other spontaneous forms of collective force, each created

---

[1] Woolsey, International Law, § 36.
[2] Meditations, VI, 44.

for a definite end and acting with various degrees of energy, sometimes very intense, but altogether without coercion." [1] Unfortunately this antithesis cannot be maintained. The distinction between the State and society lies, not in the presence or absence of coercion, but in the presence or absence of law, which is something more than mere force. Society is as coercive as any State. Entirely apart from any governmental machinery there exist forces of compulsion operating as heavily in restraint of free individual action as any legal enactment. Custom and public opinion, the laws of fashion, of honor, of morality, are all alike accompanied by coercive power. Woe to the member of any society who trangresses the received traditions of that society ; woe to the laborer who deserts his fellows in the hour of a strike or a boycott ; or to the man of fashion who outrages the customs of his set. Physical force may be absent, but banishment from a familiar circle is as real a punishment to-day as was exile from a State in the days bygone. Woe to that member of a religious community who departs from the faith of his fathers ; the hatred and scorn of former friends await him on every side ; he is deprived of most of his former associations, sometimes of the means of livelihood itself. As Locke has said, "The penalties that attend the breach of God's law some, nay, perhaps most, men seldom seriously reflect on . . . and as to the punishments due from the laws of the commonwealth, they frequently flatter themselves with the hope of impunity. But no man escapes the punishment of their censure and dislike who offends against the fashion and opinion of the company he keeps and would recommend himself to. Nor is there one of ten thousand who is stiff enough and insensible enough to bear up under the constant dislike and condemnation of his own club. . . . . This is a burden too heavy for human sufferance ; and he must be made up of irreconcilable contradictions who can take pleasure in company and yet be insensible of contempt

---

[1] Beaulieu, The Modern State, p. 51.

and disgrace from his companions."[1] The novelist may well
speak of the "inexorable laws of Mrs. Grundy."[2] Social codes
are as inexorable as were the laws of the Medes and Persians.

Public opinion, though powerful, is in many respects as
vague and indefinite as the society or societies to which it
belongs. Customs, fashions, morality itself, change from generation to generation, differ in the different strata of society,
and vary from locality to locality. Over against this must be
placed the operation of political authority. Not that political
sovereignty and public opinion are opposed at bottom. In the
last analysis they are identical. Political sovereignty is public
opinion operating by fixed method, and law differs from opinion
only in that while the one is either indefinite or particular,
possessed of indeterminate sanctions, the other is a definite
general rule of conduct enforced by a determinate authority.[3]
In this it makes for liberty.

Law does not add to the social restraints. It supersedes
them. "Freedom of men under government is to have a
standing rule to live by, common to every one of that society,
and made by the legislative power erected in it."[4] Law gives
this rule, makes explicit what was before implicit, defines the
penalties for its own violation and so, enabling men to escape
from bondage to custom, makes progress possible. Wherever
law is regularly administered the mere rules of opinion, even
those of morality, tend to sink into insignificance.[5] Subjection
to a definite law is liberty, since it protects the individual from
the interference of the 'inconstant, uncertain, unknown, arbi-
trary' opinions of society at large.

Again law defines and limits the spheres within which individuals may act, and preserves for them freedom of action

---

[1] Locke, Essay on the Human Understanding, bk. II, chap. XXVIII, § 12.
[2] Grant Allen, The Great Taboo.
[3] Holland, Jurisprudence, p. 37.
[4] Locke, Treatise on Civil Government, § 22.
[5] Clark, E. C., Practical Jurisprudence, p. 194.

within those spheres. Law, according to Sohm, determines, defines, and distributes the relations of power within the limits of human society.[1] By its own interference the State prevents interference.

Further, law is the necessary means of realizing that order which is needful for the complete development of human nature, and the realization of that perfect relation between human beings which is perfect liberty.[2] In this order and freedom coincide, and not the destruction of law, but its completion is needful for liberty. "Law in its true notion is not so much the limitation, as the direction, of a free and intelligent agent to his proper interests, and prescribes no farther than is for the general good of those. under that law : could they be happier without it, the law, as an useless thing, would of itself vanish: and that ill deserves the name of confinement which hedges us in from bogs and precipices. So that, however it may be mistaken, the end of law is not to abolish or restrain, but to preserve and enlarge freedom."[3]

Law and liberty then coincide so far as law limits the restraints of society, gives a definite rule of life, preserves for the individual freedom within definite spheres, and helps to realize the perfect development of mankind.

But though this is true, it is only half the truth. Although law in one aspect secures the liberty of the individual, and in another tends towards the realization of perfect freedom, it nevertheless endeavors to attain its end by means of restraint. By restraint law always has acted and always must. Its principle is coercive force. It does not merely direct. It commands and secures obedience by the sanction of punishment. It secures freedom in the one direction by restricting the free exercise of powers in another. It may be that those powers

---

[1] Sohm, Institutes of Roman Law, p. 14.

[2] Lorimer, Institutes of Law, bk. II, chaps. I and II.

[3] Locke, Of Civil Government, § 57.

are hurtful and injurious, due to the imperfection of human nature, none the less to the individual possessing them and desirous of using them, law comes not as liberty, but as bondage. This is the paradox of law ; though its end is liberty, its means is restraint.

Some jurists declare that might and right are identical. This is not strictly accurate, but the possession of a power does as a rule imply the possession of a corresponding right, and rights are of different kinds according to the nature of the powers from which they spring. Holland divides them into three classes.

" If a man by his own force or persuasion can carry out his wishes, either by his own acts or by influencing the acts of others, he has the " might " so to carry out his wishes.

If, irrespectively of his having or not having this might, public opinion would view with approval, or at least with acquiescence, his so carrying out his wishes, and with disapproval any resistance made to his so doing, then he has a moral right so to carry out his wishes.

If, irrespectively of his having or not having either the might or moral right on his side, the power of the State will protect him in so carrying out his wishes, and will compel such acts or forbearances on the part of other people as may be necessary in order that his wishes may be so carried out, then he has a legal right so to carry out his wishes." [1]

In these three classes of right (though Holland confines the term to the last two, they are all three rights) it is evident that there can be no permanent conflict between the second and third. That public opinion which creates the second is also, in the last resort, the sovereign power which creates the third. Whenever a conflict does occur it can only be temporary. But as between the first and third, conflicts are a matter of daily and hourly occurrence. Law and legal right exist largely to supersede and limit the exercise of that right. The power of

---

[1] Holland, Jurisprudence, p. 73.

the State is constantly employed in the attempt to curb the power of the individual. Is it possible to formulate any rule which will say to the State, "Thus far, and thus far only, oughtst thou to go "? Broadly speaking two attempts have been made to reach such a rule, one from the side of the individual, the other from that of the State, the one by determining the essential nature of the individual, the other by defining the end of the State.

The first of these is contained, scientifically, in the doctrine of a natural law, or crudely, in the mere statement of a number of natural rights. Natural Law is that body of rights which may be deduced from the essential nature of man,[1] not merely as an animal but also as an intellectual and social being.[2] These rights are primordial. They are not the creation of any State, and the State cannot take them away. They are the gift of the Creator and He alone may destroy them.[3] They are part of the very being and personality of man, the ingredients of his humanity, deprived of which he would cease to be human.

Analyzed to its last resort, the fact or power and the right are identical for the believer in Natural Law. The powers of existence and the rights of existence are the same. The only axiom of Natural Law is, " I exist as a human being, therefore I have a right to exist as a human being."[4] The fact of being involves the right to be, which in its turn involves the right to continue to be, which implies a right to the conditions of existence, and to the development of that being,[5] and so on, almost *ad infinitum*, through all the round of liberty of speech, of freedom of worship, of free locomotion, of private property,

---

[1] Lieber, Political Ethics.
[2] Hibben, The Relation of Jurisprudence to Ethics. Int. J. of E., IV, 2.
[3] Lorimer, Institutes of Law.
[4] Lieber, Political Ethics, p. 68.
[5] Lorimer, Institutes of Law.

of bequest, etc., as far, in fact, as the training, prejudices, or fancy of the philosopher may choose to carry him.

Undoubtedly a rule deduced from the essential nature of ' man, would be the greatest boon which any human being ever conferred upon his kind. But where is the being who is equal to the task? Before he can make such a deduction he must first determine exactly what is that essential nature, a task which all philosophy has vainly striven to accomplish since first γνῶθε σεαυτὸν was inscribed upon the temple of Apollo at Delphi. Who can tell exactly what is essential and common to all mankind, and how much is due to the peculiar circumstances and environment of the nation or the individual? how much the result of climate and education, or of the countless other forces operating upon the individual and producing apparently endless variation? Roughly and broadly, in certain leading characteristics and within narrow limits, we can determine the nature of man, but rules drawn from such imperfect premises must ever lack that definiteness which is at once their only utility and their sole justification.

Even if natural rights could be known, they would still be of none effect. Natural right is barren. It tells merely what is, and from it we can never pass to the what ought to be. One natural right does not involve or give rise to another natural right. The procedure which posits one right, like bare existence, for example, and then proceeds to deduce from it a whole body of other rights, is absolutely vicious. The philosopher may say, in a bold head-line, that one right does involve another, as, "The right to be involves the right to continue to be," [1] although it is somewhat difficult to see that it does so, any more than the fact (and therefore the right) of being twenty-one years of age involves a right to live to be one hundred. Examined closely, however, we find that, "the right to be consequently brings along with it a right to continue to be, which, in its duration, as in its extent, is lim-

---

[1] Lorimer, Institutes of Law, p. 213.

ited only by the power of its assertion."[1] Exactly. The power of continuing to be gives a right to continued existence so long, and only so long, as that power shall last. The power to obtain means of subsistence constitutes a right to so obtain them. The power to develop one's being is a right to such development. Each right depends on a distinct power. Between the powers there may be connection, but there is no direct connection whatever between the various rights, such that the existence of the one can be determined from the existence of the other. The existence of a natural right cannot be determined *a priori*. It is only after the power has been manifested, and the fact has happened, that the right can be known. On the basis of Natural Law, the powers manifested by an individual are the measure of his rights, whether in the struggle with the physical world, with other individuals, or with society and the State.

But the modern supporter of the doctrine is not consistent. If the power to live constitutes an inalienable right to life, why should not the power to die constitute an absolute right to death? In this respect the Stoic was the only consistent advocate of natural right. "The eternal law has decreed nothing better than this, that life should have but one entrance and many exits. Why should I endure the agonies of disease and the cruelties of human tyranny when I can emancipate myself from all my torments and shake off every bond? For this reason, and for this alone, life is not an evil, — that no one is obliged to live. The lot of man is happy because no one continues wretched but by his fault. If life pleases you, live. If not, you have a right to return whence you came."[2] To him there could be no greater stretch of tyranny than an attempt to close the doors of the only refuge from tyranny. Yet few, if any, moderns, even though they may condemn laws against suicide as inoperative, would condemn them as a violation of natural right.

---

[1] Lorimer, Institutes of Law, p. 214.   [2] Seneca, Ep. LXX.

Suicide is as much a natural right as is the right to life. If it is to be condemned it must be on the ground that it is an injury to society. Even the Stoics, while praising the act and advising its commission, admitted that it is wrong in all cases where the act would be an injury to society.[1] This is the last and greatest weakness of the doctrine of natural rights. These primordial rights, these absolute rights, these inalienable rights, are not absolute in any sense of the word. Whether they are to exist in any particular case must always be decided by an appeal to the relative argument of public expediency. Thus Professor Lorimer, in defending capital punishment, resorts of necessity to the relative argument. " Now the law which inflicts capital punishment for murder is a positive law. The natural absolute law is ' Thou shalt not kill.' That law is imposed upon us by nature, and for us, at least, it is an end in itself. The positive law which says the killer shall be killed is absolute only in so far as it tends to prevent killing, and thus to realize the natural law. It proceeds on the assumption that he who has killed once is likely to kill again ; that his example will incite others to kill ; and that killing, on the whole, will be prevented by killing him. If there be any easier and cheaper mode of vindicating the absolute law, *i.e.*, a mode in which the murderer's life can be spared without sacrificing other lives, then capital punishment is forbidden by the absolute law by which on the opposite assumption it was justified ; but that is a question which can be answered only relatively, and to which the same answer will not be always and everywhere the true one." [2]

The welfare of society is the test which determines the right to life, and so it is in connection with every other natural right ; its existence can be known, not *a priori*, but only by an examination of the circumstances of each particular case, and of its relation to the public weal. It is this which must determine

---

[1] Lecky, Hist. of Eur. Morals, p. 214 (footnote).
[2] Lorimer, Institutes of Law, p. 220.

the right, as it does, for example, in the case of freedom of
speech, a right in a tranquil, civilized community, the exercise
of which would be a crime in a mutinous garrison.

The whole phrase natural right is false and misleading in so
far as it implies that nature reveals a definite rule which might
serve to determine for the individual any absolute and invio-
lable claim to exemption from State interference in any sphere
whatever. Even when granted to exist, no deduction can be
made from it. The claim must always be based upon public
expediency. Natural right can give no definite limit for State
activity. For all practical purposes it is an idle fancy.

But while the effort to establish the individual in possession of an inalienable body of rights independent of and
superior to political authority is thus fruitless, it fares little
better with the attempt to limit the activities of the State by
defining the purposes for which it exists. Many definitions of
the end of the State may be given. For our purpose they are
pretty much of equal value. " The maintenance of security,
as well with regard to the attacks of foreign enemies as to the
danger of internal discord, constitutes the true end of the State
and must especially occupy its activity."[1] "The sole end for
which mankind are warranted individually or collectively in
interfering with the liberty of action of any of their number
is self-protection."[2] The mission of the State is to maintain the security of the individual and the nation, to determine
judicial rights, and to preserve the general conditions of existence for its people.[3] "The basis and aim of a democracy is to
avoid the desires as irrational, and to bring men as far as possible under the control of reason, so that they may live in
peace and harmony."[4] "The State has for its end the realiza-

---

[1] Von Humboldt, Sphere and Duties of Government, p. 53.
[2] J. S. Mill, Essay on Liberty, p. 22.
[3] Beaulieu, The Modern State.
[4] Spinoza, Tractatus Theologico-Polticus, chap. XVI.

tion of the best life by the individual." [1] Multitudes of similar statements might be quoted if they would serve any useful purpose, but for us they are practically valueless.

The philosopher, wishing to discover the end of the State, must find his definition ready made in his own consciousness. The definition must be an *a priori* one. It cannot be arrived at by any process of induction. The study of History does not enable the student to reach any legitimate conclusion as to what are the correct objects and the proper limitations of State activity. History only displays the objects which particular States have pursued at particular times. These objects have not been always and everywhere the same. Now war, now law, now culture, has engrossed the activities of the State. The same State in different ages pursues different ends. It curtails its activity in one direction only to increase it in another. By sumptuary laws the State of Henry VIII endeavored to regulate the lives of its people; the changes which rendered the enforcement of these laws impossible, also by the disappearance of the monasteries rendered it necessary for the State of Elizabeth to assume the administration of public charity. What was impossible for a State in one age may become possible for it in the next, and, *vice versa*, what was once wholly beyond its powers may, with changed public opinion and altered institutions, become one of its chief functions.

History shows the end for which the State was originally founded. Security or negative welfare was undoubtedly that end, but the State, like all other human institutions, is progressive, and the purpose for which it exists in civilized countries in the nineteenth century cannot be settled by appeals to the ends which it served in ancient times, or among barbarous peoples. Indeed, if these appeals were permissible, the State would be properly restricted to but one branch of negative welfare, the defense of its people against attacks from without. The State was in the beginning a military organization,

---

[1] Ritchie, Principles of State Interference, p. 102.

and as such limited its activity to the purposes for which it
had been formed. It never meddled with the private rights
and quarrels of its citizens. The chief function of the modern
State is to punish and prevent wrong. Such a conception was
unknown in primitive times. Then, private revenge was a
sacred duty. Each man was the guardian of his own household and possessions, and any injury to them was promptly
followed by reprisals. The avenger of blood was a grim reality
in those early days. But no State, however embryonic, could
be entirely ignorant of the dangerous disintegrating tendencies
of such feuds. If the State was to be preserved, these quarrels
must be repressed. Since it had neither the right nor the
power to interfere directly, the State began to act as a mutual
friend or mediator, and endeavored to secure some mitigation
of the avenger's severity. It was a distinct advance when it
was able to persuade the injured party to accept of a reason-
able compensation in lieu of a bloody revenge. Still its jurisdiction was founded on the consent of the parties. They were
free either to accept or reject its arbitration. Gradually, however, as public opinion was formed, the power of the State
increased. Little by little it became strong enough, when the
compensation was not accepted, to specify the time and nature
of the combat, to limit the quarrel to the principals alone, and,
after a time, to treat the rejection of its arbitration as an
injury to itself. If at the request of individualist philosophers
the State is to limit itself to the purpose for which it was formed,
it must divest itself not only of all those other powers which it
has gradually acquired during ages of evolution; it would have
to divest itself even of this earliest addition to its functions,
the administration of Justice. In this connection appeals to
the social life of primitive peoples are as idle as would be an
appeal to the social life of a protozoan.

Neither can any conclusions be drawn from the history of
the failures of governmental action. This is a favorite argument
with Mr. Herbert Spencer. For him it is sufficient that States
have failed to accomplish certain ends, that in particular cases

State action has been productive of evil, to decide that those cases cannot properly form objects of State activity. This argument ought, however, to take time and circumstances into account. The failures of the past are warnings to the present, not absolute prohibitions. It no more follows that, because the State has failed a hundred times to perform successfully a certain task, it must always fail, than it follows that, because one ancient emperor failed in his attempt to construct a canal across the isthmus of Corinth, the present government of Greece were wrong to complete the undertaking. With changed and improved machinery, institutions, etc., ends before impossible may now be possible. The failure of particular means to attain a certain end is not an argument against the end, it is only an argument against the means employed. The failure of a persecution does not prove that the State was wrong in trying to direct public opinion. It only proves that it was wrong in trying to direct it in that particular way. A censorship of the press may fail when education may succeed. History also shows many instances in which the State has failed, while private enterprise has been successful, but it by no means follows that these cases should, therefore, be always left to individual initiative. History shows many instances in which border raiders have conducted successful campaigns, while the armies of the State have been beaten, but it would be folly to argue that, therefore, the prosecution of a war ought to be left to private enterprise.

The truth is, the end of the State is of the nature of an ultimate and cannot be reached by any process of reasoning. Individualists are fond of comparing the State to a huge society or club, and rating it as on a par with them. The simile is not a happy one. The State is more than a voluntary and temporary organization ; it is permanent and necessary. It is not an accidental aggregation of human atoms ; it is an organism, and the units of which it is composed can only be understood by reference to it. The conception of the State is necessary to understanding the nature of man. It is the high-

est of all human institutions, and to know the end which it
actually serves would be to know, not only the end of the
Organic Will, but also the individual ends of all the units sub-
sumed under it.   On the other hand, to know the ideal end of
the State would be to know the end of life itself.   The State
is an earthly absolute.   A formulated end for it is arrived at
a priori, and has only a subjective validity.   It is neither the
end which the State does actually serve, nor yet the ideal end
toward which the State, like every progressive human institution, is gradually advancing.   It is only the conscious end, and
as such contains less than either the actual or the ideal ends.
The conscious end of the State is not a fixed or abiding one.
It is only an end for the individuals holding it.   If they are
sufficiently numerous they may constitute that public opinion
which is in the last resort the sovereignty of the State.   Those
aims which they regard as the end of the State will become
such an end, and the State will endeavor to attain them, for it
exists to perform those functions which public opinion, for the
time being, demands of it.   The realization of public opinion
for the time being is the only conscious end of the State.

   There is thus no possibility of reaching any fixed limit for
State activity, either from the side of the individual by a doctrine of natural right, or from the side of the State by estab-
lishing for it a fixed and permanent end or purpose.   Indeed,
even if an abiding end for the State were conceded as known,
it would be useless.   Just as natural right tells merely what
is, and never what ought to be, so too with the end of the
State.   Whatever end is adopted is comparatively unimportant ;
the means, direct and indirect, by which that end is to be
attained, are the important consideration.   Granted even the
narrowest end, bare security, and in the closely interwoven
web of social life, there is almost no act which cannot be inter-
preted as bearing upon that end.   Public education, sanitary
legislation, prohibition, moral legislation of all kinds, the
grossest violations of " personal liberty," of freedom of thought,
of freedom of speech, can be as readily defended from the

standpoint of mere security for life and property as from the position of the most advanced socialistic conception of the functions of the State.

The conflict is internal and irreconcilable ; liberty, in the truest and highest sense, can only be realized in a régime of law ; but law in its very nature involves restraint, and the absence of that spontaneity which is the essence of free personality. At the same time all attempts to determine "spheres" of action for individuals, *i.e.*, to divide life for them into separate departments, a department in which law must prevail and another in which liberty ought to be permitted, are useless. No such spheres can be deduced, either from the study of the nature of the individual, or from that of the constitution and purposes of the State.

CHAPTER IV.

THERE is no natural equality among men. It ought not to be necessary to say much in support of this proposition. The theory of the social contract is not more dead than is the doctrine of natural equality upon which it rested. Men are not now, and never have been, equal. Indeed, absolute equality is an impossibility. There is no equality in nature. · For two things to be absolutely equal, equal in all their parts, qualities, and relations, would be for them to be identical. Nature knows nothing of equality. No two stones, no two plants, no two animals, are ever exactly equal, and so it is with men. Men differ from one another in all their powers and capacities, both actual and potential ; they differ not only in the developed stages of their being, when moulded and formed by education and environment ; they differ also in the earliest period of existence. Even if inequalities were originally produced by artificial causes, the law of heredity operates powerfully to perpetuate them, and of that law the new-born babe is either the beneficiary or the victim. Disparities exist among the tiniest infants ; they are unlike in their inherited powers and tendencies, physical, intellectual, and moral ; their subsequent characters are not the result of individual experience alone, but are also largely the result of a race experience bequeathed by forgotten ancestors. Childhood's inequalities are at least as great as those of maturer years, extending, as they do, all the way from the precocious premature genius to the unfortunate idiot ; and from these inequalities grow naturally most of the differences of later life. Nor are children even politically equal. They are not, as Professor Huxley imagines, political zeros.[1]

---

[1] " Surely it must be a joke, and rather a cynical one, too, to talk of the political status of a new-born child." — T. H. Huxley, On the Natural Inequality of Men. Nineteenth Century, vol. XXVII, p. 9.

The infant is a personality, recognized by law, possessed of a status varying according to the status of its parents, and of rights which courts of justice will protect ; even the infant *en ventre de sa mère* is a definite legal personality; the needless destruction of its life is a crime ; while, for certain purposes of the law, it is capable of acquiring and holding property.

Great as are the disparities between individuals, as great, and for social philosophy as important, are the differences which exist in their relations one to another. Some of these differences are the direct outcome of their natural inequalities, — thus, in every group of men will be found one who, either by force of will or powers of persuasion, is the natural leader and commander of his fellows. Other relations involving inequalities, such as the relations of male and female, parent and child, old and young, are part of the order of nature and as such are necessary and independent of any social institutions. No law can make the young man of twenty equal to the man of sixty in worldly experience. No legislation can give to men the sensitiveness and emotional characteristics of women, or confer upon women the physical strength, courage, and endurance of men.

Inequalities must necessarily exist. They are not produced by the artificial conditions of life. They are facts of nature and belong to the very constitution of things. But it does not follow, on that account, that all existing inequalities are alike necessary, or that it is wise and good that natural inequalities should be allowed to work themselves out to all their legitimate conclusions. Society, the combination of men for mutual strength and benefit, is called into being for the very purpose of turning the course of nature, of making it subservient to the wants of men, of overcoming its force in one direction, by an intelligent application of its other forces in another direction. Besides this many inequalities are the result of human action, of habit and convention, and as such are entirely within the control of men and may be consciously modified by them. Because absolute equality is an impossibility, it does not therefore follow that an approximate equality is either impossible or unwise. To what extent is society or the State endeavoring to attain such an equality?

The term equality, as used by social philosophy, is an extremely indefinite one ; it may mean almost anything or nothing. It implies a comparison of two or more objects, and the relation which it expresses may consist in (1) a constant proportion between them, an equality of inequalities (2) the absence of all differences, an absolute equality, and (3) the absence of difference in respect to some particular quality. In the second of these meanings equality between men is an impossibility only demanded by an occasional fanatic in times of social disturbance. In the first it has been generally conceded to be an essential element of Justice, since first enunciated by Plato and Aristotle. That the rights of men should be in proportion to their qualities and merits, that equals should be equal, and that unequal men should remain unequal, is a position rarely questioned as an abstract proposition. But it may well be asked, of what use is it? What is its practical value? Differences existing by nature will still exist and will continue to operate despite all social institutions. Social action cannot eliminate them. Human industry can make the temperate zone as habitable as the torrid, but it is not by destroying their differences ; it cannot give to the tropics the bracing energetic life of the north, or to the north the luxuriant vegetation of the south. Social action cannot eliminate the differences of men, but it can reduce their scope and lessen their effects. As a matter of fact, society has by its interference, so modified the natural differences of men, that it would puzzle the wisest to determine, exactly, how far existing inequalities are the results of natural inequalities and how far the artificial products of social convention. Until such a determination can be reached and a standard of value obtained, the mathematical proportion of Aristotle must remain a probably true ideal without any practical value.

In themselves inequalities are neither just nor unjust. Their ethical character is derived from the part they play in social structures. A social group recognizes those qualities in men which are essential to the purposes for which it is formed. It recognizes differences in those qualities and, if it is to succeed, must take those differences into account. But as for the other qualities of its members, it has no need for them. So far as the group is concerned, they are as if they did not exist, and with regard to them the members are properly on a footing of equality, an equality of indifference. A musical club properly regards the fineness of a voice ; an athletic association, swiftness of foot ; and each distributes its honors according to the comparative excellence of its members in the qualities essential to it. This distribution will never be in an exact mathematical proportion, but the more nearly it approaches such a proportion, the more nearly will it approximate justice. But for the musical club to pay attention to the speed of its members, would be an act of injustice. So far as its purposes are concerned those other qualities are as if they did not exist, and its members are in regard to them equal with the equality of indifference, that being the only real equality between the members of any social organization.

It is not only possible, but comparatively easy to distinguish the essential from the non-essential qualities so long as only small social organizations, founded for limited and perfectly definite objects, are under consideration. The case is different when we turn to the consideration of the most complex of all social organizations, the State. If it is a hard matter to decide which of the inequalities of men are natural and which artificial, it is still harder to determine what qualities are or are not essential to the State. Before the question can be adequately answered, the end of the State must be determined; and that, as has been said already, is a problem which cannot be solved in the present unsettled condition of society. Only when this era of change is past and society has entered once more upon a stable course, will it be possible for men to agree substantially as to what is the (temporary and conscious) end of the State.

The term end of the State may be understood in three different senses. It may mean the conscious end which the State holds before itself from time to time, and which it strives to attain. Or, it may mean the ideal end which the State ought to fulfill. Most important in this connection is the actual end which the State does serve. This is not the same as the conscious end, for in all ages States have served far wider interests than those which they directly proposed to themselves. Neither is it the same as the ideal end, for human society is constantly developing and the needs of man growing, and the ideal must provide for this continuous expansion. It is not possible completely to determine the actual end of the State, for besides the end of the organic will, *i.e.*, the harmony of its members and the maintenance of law, the end of the State also includes the individual ends of all the lesser societies comprised in it, and even of the persons subject to it.[1] But we can see that among other subsidiary ends the State has attempted to curb the growth of inequality; that it has in many ways prevented the increase of disparities between its members; that it has, by repressing the free development of personality, endeavored to eliminate the differences of those subject to its influence, casting them in a common mould through education and punitory discipline. The State may not consciously aim at promoting equality. It is sufficient that in operation it does prevent, in some measure, the increase of inequalities. In pursuit of mere negative security the State has to a certain extent arranged men in a fixed order, which individual powers cannot materially alter. In the same connection it has determined spheres of individual activity, and has attempted to prevent the violation of those spheres, thus impeding the exercise of superior power, and hindering brute strength and cunning from obtaining all their natural advantages. At the same time the chari-

---

[1] Pulszky, Theory of Law and Civil Society.

table and benevolent institutions of society, hospitals, asylums, orphanages, etc., to which the State lends its aid, are all intended to lessen the effects of natural inequality.

The relations of individuals in a State may be divided into various classes. The first of these is their relation before the law. Here the rule is absolute equality. This is due to the nature of law, which is a general rule binding upon all men alike; in judicial proceedings it is the rule which is under consideration, not the qualities of the individuals; for them the .equality of indifference prevails, and personal inequalities are properly disregarded. Other relations may be divided into political, social, and industrial, but though they may thus be divided into classes, it must not be supposed that they can be separated in fact. All the relations of men are so intimately connected together that inequalities existing in one direction must, almost of necessity, produce inequalities in others. Industrial inequalities beget social, and both, political. Class distinctions existing in one department of life are of necessity carried over into every other department. How far have class distinctions been reduced by social progress?

The course of civilization has not been making towards equality. At first sight it might seem that, especially of late years, man has progressed in this direction, but even a cursory examination of the facts furnishes sufficient evidence to the contrary.

No man will claim that any tendency towards equality has been visible in the distribution of wealth. The standard of comfort does seem to have risen somewhat among the lower classes; the wage earner seems to be in a better condition than formerly, his work more constant, and his pay higher; but at the same time the wealth of the world has increased greatly, while the pauper classes in the cities have multiplied to a terrible extent. This has been the century of vast fortunes, the age of the plutocrat. It is true that the apparent disparity is exaggerated by the glaring contrasts of to-day; Fifth Avenue is not far from the slums; the millionaire and the day laborer sit side by side in the public conveyances; the merchant prince and the pauper from the tenements rub shoulder to shoulder. at the polling booths; but making all allowances for the contrasts due to social and political changes, the fact remains that the distance from the top to the bottom of the financial ladder is greater than ever before, and that the numbers at the bottom are not decreasing. At the same time, it must be admitted that with the improvements in machinery, the extension of education, the increased demand for skilled labor, and the growing intelligence of the laborers, many of the lower classes have of late years raised themselves in the social scale, while .the skilled artisans now outnumber the unskilled. Some economists go beyond this, and claim to have perceived in recent years a decided tendency towards a more equal distribution of wealth. "The diffusion of knowledge, the improvement of education, the growth of prudent habits among the masses of the people, and the opportunities which the new methods of business offer for the safe investments of small capitals:— all these forces are telling on the side of the poorer classes as a whole relatively to the richer. The returns of the income tax and the house tax, the statistics of consumption of commodities, the records of salaries paid to the higher and lower ranks of servants of government and public companies, tend in the same direction and indicate that middle-class incomes are increasing faster than those of the rich; that the earnings of artisans are increasing faster than those of professional classes, and that the wages of healthy and unskilled laborers are increasing faster even than those of the average artisan."[1] This is in England, where it can simply be said, on the other hand, the accumulated wealth per head of the population has been steadily increasing for the last two hundred years,[2] while the numbers of the poor have certainly not decreased.

---

[1] Marshall, Economics of Industry, p. 359.
[2] *Ibid.*, p. 353.

In the political relations of men, the adoption of free consti-
tutions, and the extension of the franchise, which have been
the marked features of the political development of the century, may at first sight appear to be measures tending towards
equality ; but a closer examination proves that this is not the
case. All political changes which have taken place in the past
have been merely transfers of political power from one class to
another. From king to patricians, from patricians to optimates, from optimates to the Cæsars, was the course of ancient
Rome. From nobles to burghers, from burghers to the mob,
from the mob to tyrants, was the history of most of the Italian
republics. From great feudal barons to an absolute monarch,
to a Whig aristocracy, to a commercial middle class, to the
proletariat, has been the progress of England. In no case was
the power ever really shared between two classes. So long as
social distinctions remained, the change was never the admis-
sion of a new class to equal power with an old, but was the
complete transfer of power from the old to the new. The
forms of State usage might serve for a time to hide the transfer, as they did serve to bridge over the chasm between the
two orders of administration, but the change was none the less
real. Except for brief transition periods two classes, between
whom social inequalities exist, have never shared political power
on equal terms. The emancipation of the negro has not
admitted him to equal political power with his former master.
So long as the negro and the Southern white exist as separate
social classes they never will share that power, and when the
white ceases to rule over the negro it will only be because the
negro has begun to rule over him.

In England to-day the extension of the franchise has not
produced political equality. It has only changed the political
equilibrium of the State. The moneyed middle-class are relin-
quishing their grasp upon political power, which is coming
more and more into the hands of the masses. That the influence of the lower classes has not been all-powerful is only
due to their ignorance, want of cohesion, and lack of leaders ;

but even now all political parties bid chiefly for their vote ; ministers cater to their wants and political orators strive for their favors.   To quote a writer in *The Spectator* — " The poor are flattered now for precisely the same reason that the rich were formerly.   They hold the key of all that the world values. They are not themselves able to enter on the realms of distinction, but they can admit others ; to please them is to advertise oneself ; and there is just as much temptation to see things with their eyes as there was formerly to follow the prejudices of the aristocracy, or, more recently, of the bourgeoisie." [1]   So long as class-distinctions remain within the State, so long will it be impossible for political power to be shared equally by all the citizens.

But are not the social inequalities of men gradually lessening ?   Are not the disintegration of fixed classes, and the confusion of class boundaries signs of a growing social equality ? No, the disintegration of classes is not an indication of an approaching equality.   It is merely an evidence of the ever-increasing complexity of modern society.

Classification is an intellectual necessity.   In every sphere knowledge advances only by such classification, and class arrangement is as necessary for an understanding of mankind as it is for a knowledge of the physical universe.   We cannot think of men without naturally arranging them into groups, and the social groups in which they are arranged are not arbitrarily chosen ; they are determined by natural causes. The groupings are upon the line of common qualities ; and the groups not only exist as intellectual conceptions, they exist as social realities, and social progress has consisted in a continued process of division.   Classes originally homogeneous have been divided.   The primitive horde has been broken into tribes, into families, into freemen and slaves ; the freemen gradually separated into chiefs, nobles, warriors, and so the progress has gone forward.   As the divisions of men were

---

[1] Spectator, vol. LXIV, Justice and Democracy, p. 506.

originally crude and incomplete, being based on only a few outstanding qualities, such as strength and courage, so too man's knowledge of man was incomplete. Social self-consciousness advanced *pari passu* with social division. To-day the disintegration of classes is a sign that that social self-consciousness is increasing. It does not indicate an approaching equality. It denotes increasing diversity and complexity. Fixed and stable classes with plainly marked boundaries are disappearing, and in their place are coming more and more fluctuating social groupings made upon the basis of individual personalities. Men are no longer arranged in classes determined solely, as in the beginning, by a few leading characteristics, or in classes determined, as in the later and more stable periods of development, by race and blood, family connections, hereditary offices, estates, handicrafts, etc. They are being arranged more and more in groups decided by the free exercise of the personality of the individual.

But this is not an approach to equality. Free personality is the force which above all others produces inequality. Its exercise, entirely unrestrained by custom and law, would mean that the inequalities of men would work themselves out to all their natural results. Superior cunning, superior strength, superior wisdom, would triumph over the inferior. The ignorant and the foolish would be more unequal to the wise and prudent than they are to-day when hedged around and protected by law and custom. Chief among the restraints on the free operation of personality is custom, which has been well called the centripetal power of society. The contagious influence of example holds men together. We do as others have done simply because they have done so. The example of antiquity, as expressed in habit and custom, is the conservative force in every State. It is due to its restraining influence that personality has not produced still greater diversities among men, but the present movement is significant only as it shows that custom is, for a time at least, losing its power to control the lives of men. We no longer consider it a sufficient

defence of anything to say that it is customary. Personality,
the force ever making towards inequality, is freeing itself from
the fetters of custom, and apart from custom law and morality
are empty words devoid of force, for, as Bacon has said,
"There is no trusting to the bravery of words unless it be cor-
roborated by custom."

Mr. Spencer is the leader of that group of political philosophers commonly known as Individualists. For them, liberty
for the individual is the central requisite of social progress,
and that government is the best which governs least. They
believe that all State interference should be reduced to a minimum, and, indeed, many of them indulge in shadowy dreams
of an age when all governmental interference shall entirely
cease. Liberty is the pole star by which they guide their
course. But to Mr. Spencer equality has come as a legacy
bequeathed to him by Bentham and Mill. He is unable to
free himself from the influence of his predecessors, so in his
definition of Justice he finds a place at once for equality and
for liberty, which is essentially inequality. According to him
the formula of Justice is: "Every man is free to do that which
he wills, provided he infringes not the equal freedom of any
other man." Every man should properly receive, through
free action, the rewards and punishments of his own nature,
and his liberty should only be subject to such restraints as are
necessarily imposed by the presence of other men equally free.
Justice demands an equality of spheres and an inequality of
rewards.

Mr. Spencer does not fall openly into Mill's mistake, or hold
that there are any actions of men which do not affect their fellows. Mill expressly says that there are such actions, and
claims that in regard to them men should be free from outside
interference. The lives of men, however, are not thus separa-
ble ; they are a united whole, and every action directly or indirectly affects others. But, though Mr. Spencer does not
avowedly repeat Mill's error, he falls into a mistake of his own.
He seems to imagine men as possessed of something which he

calls spheres, something which can be parceled out like ten-acre fields, which can be defined and limited, and yet within the prescribed limits of which individuals may have perfect freedom of action. The sphere of a man is at best a metaphor drawn from the material realm, and used to denote the range of his activities and influence. The spheres of individuals cannot be measured and quantitatively compared, as if they were physical entities. Nor does their extent depend upon social restrictions. The extent of an individual's sphere is the result of his powers. The man of intelligence and energy is possessed of a sphere of action vastly greater than that of the man less bountifully endowed by nature. The sphere of a man is only the powers of his personality viewed from the side of their results. When Mr. Spencer says in one place that Justice is equal freedom, and in another that it means that there should be equal spheres and unequal rewards, he states two propositions which are absolutely inconsistent. If the personality of the individual is to be free, the range of his activities and influence unchecked, spheres must be unequal. If the equality of spheres is to be maintained, the freedom of the individual must be restricted. One must choose equality or freedom. He cannot hold to both equality and freedom.

Inequality is the goal towards which Individualists are consciously working. An equality of spheres and an inequality of rewards is but an epigrammatic formula demanding, in the name of Justice, a fair field and no favors, a field in which, by free competition, every man will receive the results of his own nature; then the law of the survival of the fittest will be at liberty to perform its beneficent work, unmarred by the clumsy interference of the State. The triumph of Individualism is the triumph of inequality.

CHAPTER V.

THE conflicts have now been set forth sufficiently in detail.
In respect to liberty the State occupies a paradoxical position.
It endeavors to advance the freedom of its citizens by replacing
the vague, indefinite restraints of society by the definite restrictions of law. It tries so to mark out the bounds of individual
activity that each man may have a determinate range of action
free from unnecessary interference from others. It seeks to
further the advance of mankind towards that perfect development where order and liberty coincide. But it does all this
by means of restraint. Restraint is the mean by which the .
State strives to attain the end, liberty. In operation law
checks and curbs the free development of personality. In
every State the growth of the individual is subject to countless limitations. The law does not merely direct the citizen
as to the proper course of conduct. Its principle is coercive
force, and it compels him to yield obedience to its instructions,
and to order his life in accordance with its guidance. The
moulding influence of State power is very evident in the discipline of a reformatory, but, though less evident, it is none the
less real in every department of life. Multitudes order their
lives only by the laws of the State; for them the only question
asked, when embarking on any course of conduct, is the question, "Is it legal?" Others in a lesser degree are under the
same necessity. The conventionalities of society and the dic-
tates of the State hedge around and control every person from
the first moment of existence to the last. No man was ever
entirely beyond the restraints of law. The free development
of personality, liberty, in the truest sense, is absolutely impossible, and the law which renders it impossible does so in
the name and for the sake of liberty.

The case is similar in the matter of equality. The State has
at all times striven to lessen the natural inequalities of men.

It has always existed chiefly to overcome and limit, in certain directions, the effects of unequal powers. It was the weakness of individuals which first drove men into social union. Tribes combined into States in order to overcome the superior strength of hostile tribes. In internal affairs from the earliest ages the most important functions of the State have been the establishment of law and the administration of justice. But that administration of justice is almost exclusively confined to limiting the effects of superior strength, cunning, or craft, and to preventing unscrupulous men, deficient in social feeling, from acquiring advantages through their very defects. Law has for its fundamental motive the reduction of men to a certain fixed order. Society sprang into existence not merely to preserve the race but to preserve the weak. Apart from society, the struggle for existence operates for the preservation of the race through the triumph of the individual. Morality, *i.e.*, the customs of society, aims at the preservation of the race, through the limitation, sacrifice, and even the destruction of individuality. Yet the development of society has been accompanied by a development of the individual. Despite the action of the State the inequalities of men are steadily increasing. The extremes of wealth and poverty are growing greater. The chasm between the educated and the illiterate has been bridged over in part, but the distance which separates the savant from the boor unable to read or write, has become wider than ever. While society, the only force making towards equality, has been steadily advancing, many of its members have been advancing with it ; but many others have been standing still, or have been slowly sinking to lower and ever lower depths of degradation.

Not only is law opposed to the idea of liberty which is its only justification ; not only does the growth of inequality keep pace with the growth of the State, which exists to promote equality, but liberty and equality are themselves contradictory. Liberty involves the free development of the individual, the unfettered growth of personality. It does not imply of

necessity, dissimilarity, oddness, or eccentricity, but it does
imply originality or spontaneity.   The imposition of form from
without is inconsistent with it.   It demands expansion from
within, for self-development is the essential element of liberty.
Complete liberty is an impossibility.   The influence of parents, early education, and the customs of society are all restrictions on the self-development of the individual.   So far as
law supersedes custom it makes for liberty, but it is idle to
say that law is liberty.   The State displaces the repressive
influences of custom, the stereotyped example of antiquity, by
the milder, more regular, and more rational restraints of law,
but it none the less hinders and limits the advancement of
personality, the free growth from within as distinguished from
the moulding forces of external authority.   But it is only in so
far as law restricts personality and is thus opposed to liberty
that it in any way furthers the establishment of equality among
men.   Personality is the force ever making towards inequality.
Men are by nature unequal in all their powers, and the un-
trammeled development of the individual means the great
extension of original disparities.   Various forces, the social
feelings, customs, morality, the State and its laws, combine to
prevent such a free growth of the individual, and coöperate
through contagious example, education, and punitory discipline,
to cast men in a common mould and by a development through
external rather than internal forces, to reduce them to a common level.   Like the other social forces, law thus tends
towards equality, but in so far as it does so it is of necessity
the negation of liberty.   Liberty and equality are irreconcil-
ably opposed to each other.

This opposition between liberty and equality gives rise to
two very different ideals of Justice.   Since the internal expansion implied in liberty, and the external moulding necessitated
by equality are absolutely contradictory of each other, men are
compelled to adopt either the one or the other as the essential
element of Justice, and to view that virtue either from the side

of the individual or from that of society. From the one standpoint ideal Justice is expressed in the formula, "Each to take
according to his deserts." From the other the best statement
seems to be, "Each to receive according to his works." These
two ideals are by no means the same, and neither can be
reached from the consideration of individuals or societies at
present actually existent. Only from an ideal individual or an
ideal society can an ideal Justice be attained.

There is no such thing as a perfect individual. Men do not
live in isolation. They are bound together in countless ways,
and in the innermost being of all men there are springs of
action which impel them to union and mutual dependence.
But the philosopher, by concentrating his attention on a single
individual, is able to rise superior to the social needs of his
nature, to overlook the social instincts of men, and to regard
them as isolated beings capable of living in perfect independence. Regarding men in this manner, and leaving out of
account everything except individual personality, it is undoubtedly just that every man should take in proportion to
his deserts. At first sight this would seem to give a moral
foundation for the concept of Justice, since it rests that concept on personality, and not on things extraneous to the man,
but when the notion of desert (desert, *i.e.*, on an individualistic
basis) is analyzed this character of morality is found to pass
over into one profoundly non-moral. On a purely individualistic basis a man's desert consists in the powers of his personality plus his circumstances, or in other words in his adaptation
to his environment. Since there is no external power to
measure his merit and determine his reward, each man takes
what he can; his power of appropriation is the measure of his
desert, and the formula in all its baldness can only mean,
"Each man to take according to his strength." This was the
position of those earliest Individualists, the Sophists, when
they said that Justice is the right of the stronger.

On the other hand, when the attention is fixed upon the
State, and it is conceived of as an organism having a conscious-

ness and a will of its own, possessing aims and fulfilling purposes of its own, the individual, as an end-in-himself, is easily
lost sight of, and men become merely factors in a social progress.   That State is the most perfect which is the most fully
conscious of the end towards which it is moving and of the
means by which that end is to be attained.   In such a society
the positions of its members will be determined by their fitness
as distinguished from their desert.   Desert is a personal quali-
fication depending entirely upon the powers and circumstances
of the individual.   Fitness, on the contrary, is decided by the
powers of personality, the circumstances of the individual, and
the end of the State.   The growth of the individual is no
longer directly the object of interest; the development of the
social organism is the object of chief concern, and the attainment of that may demand that particular individuals be checked
and thwarted, turned from their natural bent, or even destroyed
altogether.   Under such conditions men would not take, by
an act of appropriation, the results of their own nature, but
would receive from the State rewards for services done on its
behalf.   At present the State is content to take men in the
positions in which it finds them; the ideal State must place
men in those positions which they are qualified to fill, and in
which it needs their services.   Negligence or defective work-
manship would be visited as an injury to the State, while faith-
ful service would be rewarded.   In a perfect condition of
affairs, where all the members of the State perform their tasks
with equal fidelity, since all the branches of work are equally
important to the organic whole, the rewards would also be
equal.   This is ideal Justice in a state of complete social solidarity; the distribution of labor according to fitness and an
equality of rewards.   Deviations from this standard of absolute
equality can only be justified as departures from the ideal,
rendered expedient in a State dealing with imperfect members.

Neither of these ideals can satisfy the majority of men.
Granted the premises from which they are deduced, and either
is sufficiently satisfactory, but only a philosopher is capable of

holding fast to either the one or the other. For most people
Justice is a varying mixture of the two. The generality of
men are not content to regard appropriation according to the
powers of individual personality as entirely just, simply because
they cannot help importing into the consideration of Justice
the idea of society and of social needs; nor can they view the
equal distribution of rewards by society according to work
done for it as constituting perfect Justice, because they are
unable to regard society as the one all-absorbing entity, and
insist upon thinking of the individual as something more than
a mere social factor, as a being of indefinite worth and an end-
in-himself. That is, men are not content to regard these
ideals simply as philosophic abstractions; they persist in attempting to apply them as real standards for existing conditions, but that is exactly what they are not and never can
become. The present is not an age either of complete individualism or of absolute social solidarity. It is an age of great
individuality, indeed, but of an individuality checked and limited by social restrictions. Society is organic, but it is not
the sole organism. The ideals are satisfactory enough as ideals,
reached from imaginary premises, but they are false when used
as standards for measuring the justice of existing conditions,
and they fail utterly when applied to the actual affairs of life.
They cannot even be used together so as to produce a third
ideal true of society as it is at present constituted, for two
false premises rarely give a true conclusion. What is needed
is a concept of Justice, not for the perfect individual alone, or
for the perfect State alone, but for the individual in the State.

The great moving force in human life is personality. Apart
from the force of individual intelligence, human institutions of
all kinds, societies of every grade and description, social clubs,
financial corporations, transportation companies, or even the
State, with its executive, legislative, and judicial machinery, must
remain entirely inoperative. It is useless, more, it is positively
injurious, to call the State propulsive, to speak of it as though

it possessed of itself some motive power by which it can advance the progress of humanity, as if it had some independent power of compulsion whereby it can reform society and elevate its citizens without the aid of or in defiance of the opposition of its individual members. The State is not propulsive; it never did and never will begin a movement of any kind; it never originated an idea either for the amelioration of the condition of its members, or for reforming its own political institutions; it has never at any time invented anything; creative power is wholly foreign to it. The only propulsive force in a State is the force of individual intelligence. We may speak of the consciousness · of the State, of its knowledge, feeling, and will, but apart from the sum total of the consciousnesses, feelings, wills, etc., of its individual members these phrases are meaningless. For the purposes of law a corporation may be held to know what its agent knows; and in the same way the State may know what its servant knows, but for the purposes of philosophy legal fictions are misleading; yet that is the only way in which that great impersonal thing, the government, can take cognizance of anything.

The moving force in society is personality. No movement, however great, but had its source in a single mind; it may change the map of a continent, decide the fate of empires and races; it may divide the world like the Reformation; but its beginning, if it could only be traced to its fountain head, would be found in the thought of a single person, a person in all probability entirely ignorant of the power and purpose of that germ idea. Such an idea spreading to other and yet other minds, becoming mixed with other ideas, undergoing strange transformations in the process, but ever growing in clearness and force as time passes on, develops at last into that mighty thing, a public opinion. This is not to say that the force of society is nothing but the sum of the individual forces which make up that society; the process is not one of simple addition; it is a cumulative one; in union the forces acquire an added power, as it were, of momentum, a power over and above the power of the individuals, and which gives to every great ' public movement its tremendous significance and its blind, unalterable course. So far as the State has any active power other than the power of its individual members, it is this "momentum," but the originating force is always individual personality.

Besides this there is another force which must be kept clearly distinct from it. The guiding force in the State must not be confounded with the power of the State. It is only within narrow bounds that the progress of the State can be guided at all. The very quality of State force which enables us to describe it as "momentum," serves to render its direction fixed and permanent, and lends to great public movements that appearance of blind fatality which always characterizes them. Such as it is, however, the guiding or governing force is always in the hands of definite persons, and so far as the State is subject to intelligent direction, it is under the control of individual minds. If by the sovereign power we understand the power of the State, that power must always reside in the mass of the people of the State, but when we use that term to denote the directing and governing intelligence, it is rightly described, as by Austin, as residing in the minority. Louis XIV was not insane with arrogance when he identified himself with the State ; he recognized himself as being the governing intelligence, and living in a time when the absence of any great social convulsion rendered that power more wide-reaching than usual, he easily overlooked the real moving force of the State and concluded that the guiding power was all in all, a mistake which his unfortunate descendant was not likely to make amidst the flood-tide of the Revolution. But whether in the directing, or in the moving power, the originating force is alike personality. Apart from individual intelligence the State in all its branches, legislative, executive, and judicial, and society in all its varied combinations, are absolutely dead. Personality is the only creative force.

Beyond this power of individual intelligence, however, the State possesses another great force, one which is not due to personality, and which may be described as the force of inertia. The State is the great conservative power. In society with its customs, and the State with its laws, human life has assumed a settled form, and, as it were, crystallized. No power on earth can, either suddenly or materially, alter that form. Changes can only arise as the result of long ages of gradual development. The past decides the present, and the present rules the future. When we consider human life as a whole, there is no simile quite so expressive of the truth as that of a mighty river, flowing in a definite direction, with fixed and immovable bounds ; individuals have their places in the stream, and must drift with the current. All their lives long men are limited and confined by social necessities ; possessing natures capable of expansion in many directions, they are so hedged round by circumstances that they can only obtain a forced and artificial growth in predestined ways ; individuals are compelled to conform to the limits fixed by society. The State, as the highest organization of society, aims directly at the preservation of those limits. The State resists all change. In all its functions, in every branch of its activity, it operates to preserve the natural expectation of men, and that natural expectation is nothing but the belief that what is will always be. Even when in its legislative capacity the State apparently introduces changes, it is in reality only registering changes already undergone, or amending laws rendered useless by the altered conditions of society. The State, as the organ of conservation, is constantly using its power to repress individuality, but it cannot do so completely, for personality is the source of all its activity, and the most tyrannical government must at least foster the individuality of its instruments of oppression.

This is the great conflict, the conflict between personality, the force of change and progress, on the one hand, and on the other the State, the power making towards permanence and stability. For existing society, Justice can consist neither in the triumph of the individual, nor in the attainment of a complete social solidarity. The progress of humanity has been an oscillation between these two extremes, and if an objective standard of Justice is ever to be obtained, it must be by determining the middle course which that progress is pursuing.

This conception of society, or the State, as a negative or limiting power, and of individual personality as the only positive and active force, may seem to be purely fanciful, or forced and artificial, but it is in reality an opposition at the basis of all law. The complete separation of the individual and the State is possible only in thought and as mere abstractions; to no single instance can we point and say, "this is due to the action of the individual alone," or "to the action of the State alone"; everything in life is the resultant of the two. An analysis of the notion of a right furnishes evidence of this. There is no such thing as a natural right springing from the nature of the individual alone, nor any such thing as a right created by the State.

Right and might are said to be identical. Right rests upon man's power to choose and will, upon his tendency to appropriate things, and to refer to himself things outside of himself. Its foundation is power, and the conception of it as power over an object is the only perfectly definite jural conception.[1] Right is based upon the force of personality, the power of will, which will may be either the will of the individual or the will of the whole community. With this conception of right it is easy to understand the somewhat paradoxical maxim of law that common error, or, as it is sometimes read, common opinion, makes right. Since right is the universal will, or the will of the community as a whole, it matters not whether that will expresses truth or error, it is equally right for all who are subject to it, and this is not merely a theoretical position; it is a position upon which courts of law stand daily in matters of practice. Further, under such a conception it is plain that no individual can have an absolute right to anything, and this,

---

[1] Puchta, Outlines of Jurisprudence as a Science of Right.

too, is a fundamental position of the law. It is only upon
this view that right is founded upon power, and absolute rights
are impossible, that the various statutes of limitations are de-
fensible. All that a statute of limitations means is, that a
person who has long neglected to exercise the power or domin-
ion of his will over certain objects, will not be allowed to
resume that power to the prejudice of others. And not to
multiply instances of how this principle operates, it is due to
this conception of right that bare possession obtains such
force in courts of law.

But although power is the source of right, it must not be
identified with it. Such a conception is shocking to the moral
sense of mankind. For the majority of men a right is power
exercised in particular ways according to some more or less
hazy notion of a rule. Thus Whewell defines a right as being
that "which, being conformable to the supreme rule of human
action, is realized in society and vested in a particular person." [1]
If power alone can constitute a right, it is only a natural right,
and natural rights are possible only in the impossible state of
nature. In society all rights are artificial.

Rights may be classified according to the powers from which
they spring. Thus Holland, after defining a right as "one
man's capacity of influencing the acts of another, not of his
own strength, but of the opinion or force of society," [2] proceeds
to divide rights (in a passage quoted above) into three classes,
according as the power from which they arise is that of the
individual, of public opinion, or of the State. To the first of
these he declines to apply the term right at all, designating it
simply, might. The second constitutes moral right, and the
third, legal right. If these classes are to be regarded as indicating the changes which take place with the addition of new
powers, they are correct enough ; but if they are to be viewed
as mutually exclusive, and as existing independently of each

---

[1] Whewell, Elements of Morality, bk. I, § 84.

[2] Holland, Jurisprudence, p. 70.

other, the division is absolutely bad. Holland evidently regards them as independent, for he speaks of a man having a moral right, "irrespectively of his having or not having the might," and of his having a legal right "irrespectively of his having or not having either the might or the moral right on his side." Legal rights do not exist in independence of moral rights, nor does either of them exist apart from the power of personality. In a legal right there is an element of power not in the moral right, but it is simply the moral right rendered definite and enforced by the action of the State. The State does not create legal rights without regard to moral rights; it endeavors to register public opinion, and its power is at bottom only a particular application of the power of that public opinion. Whenever social changes have divorced legal right from moral right, the separation has been but temporary, and is due only to the slowness with which the formulated decrees of society alter as compared with unformulated public opinion. Further, neither legal right nor moral right exists apart from personal power. Every right, whether legal or moral, presupposes a capacity inherent in the person who is the subject of such right. Public opinion and the State do not confer upon the individual any new powers not already his by nature. What they do do is to enable him to exercise his natural powers in particular ways, free from the interference of others. The natural power is not of itself the right, but it is an essential element in the right. In no sense of the word can the sick man be said to have a right to the benefits of health, the blind man to sight, or the deaf man to the pleasures of music. The majority of legal rights depend upon bare personality, but they are continually modified by the condition of the individual; thus the sick man may be quarantined to prevent infection, may be restrained by hospital authorities, or if his trouble is mental may be confined in an asylum, while if the personality itself fails, either through a natural or a civil death, all rights dependent upon it cease also.

Personality is the source of all activity, and, therefore, of all

rights ; but it cannot be said that personality makes rights any
more than it can be said that the State creates them.   Personality limited and defined is right ; if by society at large, it is
moral right; if by the State, it is legal right.   Personality
itself gives no right, but it supplies the power or capacity
which is presupposed in the right.   The State adds nothing to
the powers of personality.   Sir Vernon Harcourt is credited by
an American newspaper with saying, "Nature gives no man
power over his earthly goods beyond the term of his life.   The
right of a dead hand to dispose of his property is a pure creation
of the law, and the State has the right to prescribe the conditions and the limitation under which that power shall be exercised." [1]   No "dead hand" ever did, or ever will, dispose of
property.   A living man makes a disposition of property to
take effect upon the event of a future contingency, and the
State guarantees that, when that contingency has happened,
the disposition so made shall be carried into effect.   A man
may, by deed of gift, vest certain properties in a trustee to be
disposed of in certain ways upon the fulfilment of certain conditions, and the State will enforce the due performance of the
trust even if the grantor be no longer in the land of the living.
A will goes into effect only on the death of the testator, but it
is not the work of a "dead hand" ; it is a trust created by a
living man dependent upon a future contingency, his own
death.   The State adds nothing to the powers of personality,
but it limits them, prescribes the ways in which they are to be
exercised, and by imposing limitations on other persons makes
their free exercise possible.   The standard according to which
the limitations are imposed is the public welfare.   The right
of property, for example, rests first on the individual power of
appropriation, and second, on the limitations which the State
has fixed for such power.   Where the public welfare demands
it, the power may be still further restrained, as in the case of
owners of property required for roads, railways, and other pub-

---

[1] Scottish American, June 27, 1894.

lic purposes, and the individual loses at once all rights, moral or legal, beyond the new limits imposed by social expediency.

The law is thus essentially negative. This characteristic of the law appears in a multitude of ways. Leaving out of account the discussion as to whether the law cares for the negative or the positive welfare of the individual, it may be said in the first place that the law is negative in its structure. To quote a great Australian jurist : " It is remarkable that in all modern law, there is no distinct statement of men's general duties.. It might reasonably be expected that such a record in plain and unambiguous terms would be found in the front of every national system of law. Yet as Mr. Justice Markby (*Elements of Law*, p. 74) observes, there is no country in which we have on official authority a complete category of duties. The law invariably takes the shape of penalty. It does not command its subjects to do certain acts or observe certain for- bearances. What it says is, that if any person does or forbears to do such and such acts he shall undergo such and such a punishment. There is no direct command, and the primary object of the legislator's regard is that which is really subsid- iary — the sanction. The duty is always assumed to be known ; and its definition must be extracted from the penalty annexed to its violation." [1]

Further, except in a few cases, such as the granting of writs of injunction or decreeing specific performance, courts of law and equity are almost wholly occupied in remedying or pun- ishing wrongs done. Although the end of all punishment is the prevention of future wrongs, the law attempts to gain that end indirectly, and the courts do not as a rule interfere until the wrong has been done. Indeed the great body of the law may be almost divided according to the nature of the wrong done, such as wrongs arising from contracts; torts, or wrongs independent of contract; and wrongs against the public, or crimes. Jural Justice is remedial and preventive, but how far

---

[1] Hearn, Aryan Household, p. 403.

it is the one and how far the other is by no means clear. It is evident that in the case of crimes the punishment is never remedial, and that in civil proceedings it is not wholly so. Thus A and B enter into a contract which B breaks; the court awards damages to A; the award to A is more than a remedy for the wrong done, and is intended to operate to prevent future breaches of contracts, while allowing the successful litigant costs is plainly a punishment of the defeated party. One thing is certain, jural justice, whether preventive or remedial, is usually founded on wrongs done and is negative in its operation.

The nature of law is essentially negative. The maxim, *Salus populi suprema lex*, does not mean that public welfare is the basis of rights, but that it is the standard for limiting them. When the safety of the community demands it, the rights of the individual must give way. A common notion, which belongs properly to Asiatic countries, is that courts exist to administer justice : in reality they exist to administer law; whether that law is in accord with Justice is a question for legislators, not for judges. It, however, happens occasionally that cases arise upon which the law is silent ; at such times, despite judicial fictions, the judges are compelled to act in a legislative capacity and to make law. Mr. Justice Willes thus laid down the principles which should guide them : " It could only be done on principles of private justice, moral fitness, and public convenience, which when applied to a new subject make common law without a precedent."[1] Chief Baron Pollock commenting upon this passage said, " My Lords, I entirely agree with the spirit of this passage, so far as it regards the repressing what is a public evil and preventing what would become a general mischief ; but I think there is a wide difference between protecting the community against a new source of danger and creating a new right. I think the common law is quite competent to pronounce anything to be illegal which is manifestly

[1] Millar *vs.* Taylor, 4 Burr, 2312.

against the public good; but I think the common law cannot create new rights and limit and define them, because in the opinion of those who administer the common law such rights ought to exist according to their notions of what is just and right and proper." [1]

The welfare of society is a negative principle, employed not as the foundation of, but for the limitation of the rights of the individual. Rights arise from the powers of personality as circumscribed and defined by the action of the State. In society as it exists at present a right is never either a natural power or a purely artificial creation of the State ; it is always a State limitation of personality.

It is impossible then to formulate, either from the study of the nature and functions of society as a whole, or from the consideration of man as an individual personality and end-in-himself, an ideal of Justice which will be true for existing conditions. The correct ideal of Justice cannot exist in liberty, the freedom of self-development, and the right of men to take in proportion to their powers, nor yet in equality, the claim of all the human units of' society to the same treatment and the same reward for work done for the State. Individualism and socialism, so far at least as they are scientific theories of government and claim to be founded on principles of Justice, are the results of one-sided and partial views of the facts of existence. On the one hand, man is not a self-sufficient being leading a solitary existence or living for himself alone, nor, on the other hand, is he merely a member of a higher organism. The individual serves the social organism of which he is a member, but at the same time he is more than a member of that organism, and the organism serves him, and it is impossible to say that the individual is above society, or that society is above the individual, for in certain aspects each proposition is true.

---

[1] Jeffreys *vs.* Boosey, 4 H. L. 936.

The moral life of man has a dual character which pervades every sphere of morality. Every action which is possessed of moral quality has both an individual and a social aspect, and there is no such thing as a human action which "chiefly concerns society" or one which "affects the individual alone"; neither can the virtues be divided into individual and social, for every virtue demands for its existence the individual personality and the social environment, and possesses in equal measure effects purely personal to the actor and results of interest to the public. The virtue of Justice is not a social virtue any more than it is a personal one; it is the product of personality in society, and cannot be determined by the study of either the individual or society alone. It is the chief merit of Mr. Spencer's treatment of Justice that he recognized the presence and claims of both factors, while its great defect is the artificial manner in which those factors are united. Mr. Spencer regards, as the primary and positive element of Justice, the right of the individual to take in proportion to his powers. This is a law of all life, and if men lived absolutely alone, they would thus receive only the rewards and punishments of their own natures. But men do not live alone, and the presence of others circumscribes the individual and imposes limits upon him. This is the negative element. The individual should still be free to receive the rewards and punishments of his own nature, but that freedom ought to be limited by the like freedom to all, and the formula of Justice becomes: Every man is free to do that which he wills, provided he infringes not the equal freedom of any other man. Mr. Spencer rightly recognizes the positive and negative characters of these elements of social life, the powers of personality and the limitations imposed by social organization, but he is wrong in separating them, and referring the social limitation alone to the sphere of the activity, leaving the individual powers to determine the reward of action. Men in a state of absolute individuality undoubtedly would take each in proportion to his powers of appropriation, and the addition of others would limit the range of this appropriation *de facto*, but it would only limit it *de jure* if there was organic union, and not mere accumulation or multiplication of numbers. Acknowledge an organic union of men, and the only excuse for demanding an equality of spheres, the mechanical division of the chances of existence among a number of individuals, vanishes, for then the spheres of the members of the organism are properly determined by the needs of the organism, which needs may or may not demand equality. The mere presence of more than one member in an organism gives no claim to the equal division among such members of the chances of continued existence, such as might arise from the concourse of a mob of independent units. Mr. Spencer falls into a greater mistake in separating sharply the positive element of individual life from the negative element of social organization, making the first alone determine the reward, and the second the sphere of action. This is the result of the same artificial and arithmetical conception of society which has just been noticed. Correctly, both the positive element of personality and the negative element of social limitation must enter at one and the same time into every realm of human life, and it is impossible to point to any fact and say, "This is the product of the powers of the individual," or "This is the result of the restraints of society." In the organic society every part is determined at once by both factors. The sphere of a man is not, and never will be, something which may be calculated, determined, and hedged around by society; it must always be affected by the powers of the individual, and will vary as those powers vary, as well as with the changing bounds imposed by social restrictions. In the same way the reward of action cannot properly be left to the inequalities which result from the differences of individual powers where men are all given a fair field and no favors. That might be right were society non-organic, but as things are, the social organism is interested in, and does as a matter of fact interfere with, the results achieved by its individual members. The conception of Justice which would leave the reward of action to be determined solely by the powers of the actor, and would relegate social interference entirely to the sphere of activity, is grossly inaccurate, since in the organic society as it is actually consti-tuted social limitations and personal powers together decide both the spheres occupied and the results attained by men.

Separate the powers of the individual and the social re-straints and it is an easy task to assign definite functions to them. By thus dividing them Mr. Spencer readily arrives at a set formula of Justice. The process, however, is radically vicious. The two factors of moral life cannot be separated; nothing is the product of either the one or the other, but the two forces are necessarily united in every branch of life. It is not easy to determine what are the precise functions of each when the two are in combination. It is a difficult matter to say what in any resultant is due to the one or the other, but until the part played by each force is determined, no formula of Justice can be reached. What restraints ought to be placed upon the powers of personality? What should be the limits of State interference, the bounds of the social restrictions? The State as the organ of permanence checks and curbs indi-viduality, the force making towards growth and change, and its restrictions of the powers of the individual are what consti-tute rights. Yet the State can never completely repress the forces of personality, for the very power employed to restrain individual personality is collective personality. Before we can say exactly what is and what is not just, a rule must be formu-lated which will serve to determine how far the State power ought to limit and confine the individual power. Analysis alone cannot produce such a formula of Justice.

The study of history cannot furnish it. Mr. Spencer de-scribes the progress which history displays to us, as a 'ten-dency to individuation.' He says: "In man we see the highest manifestation of this tendency. By virtue of his com-plexity of structure he is furthest removed from the inorganic world, in which there is least individuality. Again his intelli-gence and adaptability commonly enable him to maintain life to old age — to complete the cycle of his existence ; that is, to fill out the limits of his individuality to the full. Again he is self-conscious, that is, he recognizes his own individuality. And as lately shown even the change observable in human affairs is still towards a greater development of individuality — may still be described as 'a tendency to individuation.' " [1] In the triumph of perfect individualism, perfect morality and perfect life will be realized. The movement, however, is a complex one, involving as it does greater and greater union, and at the same time ever-increasing separation. The process of individuation is one of universal specialization, the growth of diversities, and implies as a corollary the constant increase of mutual dependence, while at the same time the development of specialization demands freedom and involves separation. History furnishes abundant evidence of progress as the advance towards individuation, but it nowhere shows any tendency towards Individualism as implied in the theory of government so called. The development of the individual has been an inner growth, a development of self-consciousness, a growth in power produced, not through the removal of outward restraints, but through the development of the inner life. The freedom of the individual has been increased, not by the decay of State interference, but by the progress which society itself has made. The individual has grown in self-consciousness, but so has society. Increased complexity and a better adaptation of means to ends mark the advance of the State. To this and to the development of the powers of personality, and not to any decrease in State interference, is due the apparent increase in the liberty of the individual. Social solidarity is no longer the crude and unyielding thing it was in the dawn of civilization, but it is none the less as real, and State interference has suffered no diminution in the progress of the ages. Indeed the very development of the social organism makes social solidarity greater to-day than ever before. The increas-

---

[1] Social Statics, p. 259.

ing complexity of life makes society more than ever one and ever and ever adds to the inter-dependence of its members. History can never arbitrate between the individual and the State.

Rising above the plane of mere process, and endeavoring to interpret the progress of society teleologically, a formula of Justice might be reached, if the end of the State could be determined. The principle upon which State interference is consciously applied is public welfare. But public welfare is meaningless apart from some conception of the end of the State. If the phrase is taken to mean only the aimless preservation of being, the purposeless continuation of the existence of the State, it is empty and devoid of all content. If public welfare is to be employed as a standard for determining the rights of individuals, it must be conceived as the welfare of a State possessing certain aims and striving to advance towards a definite goal. The end of the State may be used in three different meanings. It may mean the end which a State from time to time places consciously before itself. It may mean the end which the State does actually as a matter of fact fulfill ; and it may also mean those functions which the State ought to and will serve in a more advanced stage of development. The conscious end of the State will not suffice, for the standard must be used as a test of that end. Neither will the actual end served by the State be enough, for the State is continually developing and the end of to-day will not be an adequate end for to-morrow. The end of the State which is to furnish the ideal of Justice must itself be the ideal end.

The State is an earthly absolute. Its end is not merely the formal end, the establishment of harmony amongst its members ; it comprises also the ends of all the individuals and of all the minor social organisms contained in it, and this, not merely as they are, but as they will become in a continually developing humanity. To know the end of the State would be to know the end of all life. Such a knowledge cannot be reached by any rational process ; it transcends our experience and is metaphysical in its character. From the earliest times of which we have any historical evidence down to the schism of the Reformation, the basal concept of society was a metaphysical one. The State was theocratic ; upon a belief in an overruling intelligence and purpose, a theory of divine government, the relations of individuals to each other and to the State were regulated, and upon that foundation law and rights directly rested. However inadequate for scientific purposes, the theory furnished a metaphysic of society sufficient for the needs of the moment, and upon which the current ideals of Justice were based. With the seventeenth century began the attempt to rationalize the State. For two hundred years men have been striving to attain a rational conception of society and have failed. The theory of artificial making was entirely unequal to explain the social phenomena, and now the conception of society as an organism is felt to be inadequate. This Mr. Ritchie has seen. " Because the conception of an organism is more adequate to society than the conception of an artificial compound, it does not follow that it is wholly adequate. We have just seen that a one-sided application of organic growth leads to difficulties as well as the conception of artificial making. These we can only escape by recognizing a truth which includes them both. We must pass from organism to consciousness, from Nature to the spirit of man." The truth is, the attempted rationalization of society is a failure, and before we can understand the State we must return to a social metaphysic. It is impossible on a purely rationalistic basis to explain the individual life, more impossible still to explain that entirety of life which constitutes the State. Until a social metaphysic has been constructed, no ideal of Justice, true for existing conditions, can be attained, and the majority of men will continue to oscillate between the two false ideals based upon the impossibilities of perfect individuality or of complete social solidarity. As men incline to the one extreme or the other, they will hold things to be just or unjust, according to either the standard of Individualism, "to each in pro-

portion to his deserts," or the formula of socialism, "to each
according to his work (or needs)." As such, the ideal of Justice is purely subjective, binding only upon the individual holding it, and not applicable as a test of the rightness or wrongness
of any existing conditions. Society is an inexplicable ultimate
from which no concept of Justice possessing objective validity
can be deduced.

BIBLIOGRAPHY.

Aristotle. Politics, Nicomachean Ethics.

Austin. Lectures on Jurisprudence.

Beaulieu. The Modern State.

Bentham. Principles of Morals and Legislation.

Bluntschli. Theory of the State.

Burlamaqui. Natural and Politic Law.

Clark, E. C. Practical Jurisprudence.

Dante. De Monarchia.

Denis. Théories et Idées morales dans l'Antiquité.

Donisthorpe. Individualism, a System of Politics.

Engels. Socialism, Scientific and Utopian.

Fabian Essays.

Fowler. Principles of Morals.

Fustel de Coulanges. La Cité Antique.

Humboldt, W. von. The Sphere and Duties of Government.

Hearn. Aryan Household.

Hobbes. Leviathan. Philosophical Elements of a True Citizen.

Holland. Jurisprudence.

Hume. Essays.

Kant. Philosophy of Law.

Lacy. Liberty and Law.

Lecky. History of European Morals.

Lieber. Political Ethics.

Letourneau. Property, its Origin and Development.

Lightwood. Nature of Positive Law.

Lorimer. Institutes of Law.

Locke. Essay on the Human Understanding. Of Civil Government.

Leibnitz. Codex Diplomaticus Juris Gentium.

Maine. Ancient Law. Early History of Institutions.

May. Democracy in Europe.

Miller. Philosophy of Law.

Mill, J. S. Utilitarianism. Essay on Liberty.

Montesquieu. Spirit of Law.

More. Utopia.

Plato. Republic. Statesman. Laws.

Pollock. Essays in Jurisprudence and Ethics.

Puchta. Outlines of Jurisprudence as a Science of Right.

Pulszky. Theory of Law and Civil Society.

Reid, Thos. On the Active Powers of Man.

Ritchie, D. G. Darwinism and Politics. Principles of State Interference. Equality (Contemporary Rev., Oct. 1892).

Rousseau. The Social Contract. Discours sur l'Origine et les Fondemens de l'Inégalité parmi les Hommes.

Sandars. Institutes of Justinian.

Schmoller. Idea of Justice in Political Economy.

Sidgwick. Methods of Ethics.

Sohm. Institutes of Roman Law.

Spencer, H. The Man versus the State. Justice. Social Statics.

Spencer, H. and others. A Plea for Liberty.

Spinoza. Ethics. Tractatus Theologico-Politicus.

Stephen, J. F. Liberty, Equality, and Fraternity.

Stephen, Leslie. Science of Ethics.

Schaeffle. Quintessence of Socialism.

Tarde. Transformations du Droit.

www.ingramcontent.com/pod-product-compliance
Lightning Source LLC
Chambersburg PA
CBHW031443270326
41930CB00007B/844

9 7 8 3 3 3 7 8 5 8 6 8 1